BIRDWATCHING LONDON

David Darrell-Lambert is Director of the consultancy Bird Brain UK, and undertakes bird surveys all over London for a variety of clients. He also regularly gives talks on birding and leads guided birding walks in the capital. He lives with his family near Rainham Marshes RSPB reserve.

www.birdbrainuk.com

CONTENTS

ACKNOWLEDGEMENTS

First I would like to thank Ms Anderson from Bruce Grove Junior School, Tottenham, for taking our class to Rye House RSPB reserve back in the late 1970s, which ignited my passion for birds.

During the course of this book my wife Denise has helped endlessly in various ways, including keeping me sane, trying to keep me organised, being so accommodating on all the days when I suddenly said, 'It's nice weather tomorrow, so OK if I go off and take pictures for my book?', always encouraging me to challenge myself, not least by doing this book, and supporting me over the many years I have been obsessed with birds.

Also thank you to my two lovely daughters, Mia and Sophie, for their support, being OK when I'd go missing, and coming with me on some of my many research trips across the capital.

Many people have helped me with this book by taking me to their local patch and giving me lots of information to help me write it. They are: Chris Farthing (Woodberry Wetlands), Susan Huckle (Waterworks Nature Reserve), Tony Brown (Wanstead Park and Flats), Steve Bacon and Alan Bell (Fairlop Waters Country Park), John Archer and the regulars on the Bird Barmy Army walks (Victoria Park), Bob Watts (Tower Hamlets Cemetery), Dave McGough (Hornchurch Country Park & Ingrebourne Hill), Richard Green and John Bushell (Greenwich Peninsula Ecology Park), Joe Beale (Greenwich Park), Lev Parikian (Crystal Palace Park), John Birkett (South Norwood Country Park), David Campbell and Peter Alfrey (Beddington Farmlands), Derek Coleman (Morden Hall Park), my very good friend Des McKenzie (Hyde Park and Kensington Gardens), Tony Duckett (The Regent's Park), Richard Bullock (London Wetland Centre WWT), the man himself Franko Maroevic (Richmond Park), Charlie Farrell (Wormwood Scrubs), Alan Cheeseman, Andrew Peel and Diana Housley (Bedfont Lakes Country Park), Rob Innes (Staines Reservoir), Ian Bennell (Cassiobury Park), Robert Callf (Grovelands Park), Pete Mantle (Hampstead Heath), Phil Vines (William Girling Reservoir), Adam Wilson (River Lee Country Park), Neville Smith (King George V Reservoirs) and Peter Lambert (Walthamstow Wetlands).

Also thanks to Dave Morrison for passing on some of his vast knowledge on Peregrines to me, Philippa Barr for her keen eyes, Mathew Frith of London Wildlife Trust and Stephen Moss for their help, and the many people I have spoken to over the years about their local patches all over London.

There were also lots more people who helped me, but we just didn't have enough space to include their local areas as well. They are: Bob Watts (Alexandra Palace Park), Robert Callf (Trent Park), Peter White (Wandsworth Common and Tooting Bec Common), Vince Halley-Frame and Steve Blake (Dagenham Chase Nature Reserve) and Magnus Andersson (Brent Reservoir).

Page 1: Cormorant on the Thames by the London Eye.

Page 2-3: Highgate Pond at Hampstead Heath.

Page 4: Mute Swan at Rainham Marshes.

FURTHER INFORMATION

For bird identification guides, the best is the *Collins Bird Guide* by Lars Svensson and Killian Mullarney (Collins); a cheaper alternative is the *RSPB Pocket Guide to British Birds* by Simon Harrap (Bloomsbury Natural History).

Through his extensive media work David Lindo has helped to put urban birding on the map. His two books are: *The Urban Birder* and *Tales from the Concrete Jungle: Urban Birding Around the World* (Bloomsbury Natural History).

OPTICS (BINOCULARS & TELESCOPES)
In Focus, London Wetland Centre, Barnes, www.at-infocus.co.uk

USEFUL WEBSITES
London Wildlife Trust: www.wildlondon.org.uk
RSPB (Royal Society for the Protection of Birds): www.rspb.org.uk
Wildfowl and Wetlands Trust: www.wwt.org.uk
London Bird Club: www.londonbirders.wikia.com
London Natural History Society: www.lnhs.org.uk
The Urban Birder (David Lindo): www.theurbanbirder.com
Marylebone Birdwatching Society; www.birdsmbs.org.uk
Essex Wildlife Trust: www.essexwt.org.uk
www.londonperegrines.com
www.london-peregrine-partnership.org.uk
www.blackredstarts.org.uk
www.wildlifetrusts.org
www.royalparks.org.uk
www.woodberrywetlands.org.uk
www.walthamstowwetlands.com

And for Waxwing sightings, on Twitter: @waxwingsuk

PICTURE CREDITS
All photographs by David Darrell-Lambert except pages

1	Beata Moore, Alamy Stock Photo
9	London Wildlife Trust
13	Malcolm Park, Alamy Stock Photo
14-15	Helen Babbs, London Wildlife Trust
18 top	Don Lewis, London Wildlife Trust
26	Tony Brown
29	Stuart Melvin, Alamy Stock Photo
41	Tomos Brangwyn
47	David Tipling, Getty Images
52 bottom	Graham Coster
67	Patricia Phillips, Alamy Stock Photo
77 bottom left	James Cracknell, London Wildlife Trust
78 left	Krisz Feteke, London Wildlife Trust
79 top	D. Greenwood, London Wildlife Trust
84	Mathew Frith, London Wildlife Trust
85 top	Mathew Frith, London Wildlife Trust
108-9	Graham Coster
129 top	Mathew Frith, London Wildlife Trust
155	Eric Hosking, FPLA, Alamy Stock Photo
165	Louise Murray, Alamy Stock Photo
174-5	Tim Webb, London Wildlife Trust
177	Mathew Frith, London Wildlife Trust
178 bottom	Russell Hayes
185 top	James Cracknell, London Wildlife Trust

INTRODUCTION

Birdwatching in a city does not always strike people as an obvious thing to do.

In fact, it can be significantly easier to see wildlife up close in an urban setting than a rural one. Potential prime real-estate for birds might be a new nest site in a street light, or a mighty oak tree in the local park. London, indeed, is one of the greenest of cities – and bluest: it is full of lakes, rivers and canals, too. Birds descend in their thousands to our concrete jungle for somewhere to rest after long journeys from a distant country, or a place to call home and raise a family.

So why are London's birds often so tame? Well, they have to be! Hyde Park on a sunny day will attract thousands of visitors: the birds don't have the luxury of waiting for everyone to leave before feeding. No, the trees are full of hundreds of caterpillars, and the families of Blue Tits will pile in while we're boating on the Serpentine oblivious to the wildlife around us.

So imagine, then, the natural abundance in the capital's many nature reserves, from beautifully small Camley Street around the back of Kings Cross to colossal Rainham Marshes alongside the Thames on the east side of town. Whether you spend an hour at one, or most of a day at another, there are wonderful birds to be seen around London.

I was raised in Tottenham, and my father and I started to look for birds in Tottenham Cemetery. We discovered that Wood Warblers and Pied Flycatchers regularly migrated through it. So if we found those kinds of bird in Tottenham Cemetery, you should be able to discover your small piece of bird heaven somewhere in London.

Here in this guidebook, then, are plenty of places to visit. You may find yourself discovering your own local patch – somewhere you'd never thought of going to watch birds. Have fun. . .

David Darrell-Lambert
May 2018

This book does not claim to be an exhaustive guide to all the places around Greater London that are worth visiting to watch birds, only to provide a wide geographical range of those sites the author has found to be particularly worth visiting.

Basic visitor information – opening times, nearest Tube or railway station – is provided for each destination included. Rather than giving what are in many cases very long weblinks, we suggest you use Google to take you to the website for each site to find comprehensive information on everything from detailed directions to disability access. Websites for the principal conservations etc. are given on the last page. Please note that some reserves will charge an admission fee to non-members.

LONDON'S BEST BIRDWATCHING SITES

1	Woodberry Wetlands	20	St James's Park
2	Waterworks Nature reserve	21	Hyde Park & Kensington Gardens
3	Wanstead Park & Flats	22	The Regent's Park
4	Fairlop Waters Country Park	23	Holland Park
5	Victoria Park	24	London Wetland Centre
6	Tower Hamlets Cemetery	25	Richmond Park
7	Hornchurch Country Park & Ingrebourne Hill	26	Wormwood Scrubs
8	Rainham Marshes	27	Bedfont Lakes Country Park
9	Southend-on-Sea	28	Staines Reservoir
10	East India Dock Basin	29	Cassiobury Park
11	Greenwich Peninsula Ecology Park	30	Grovelands Park
12	Greenwich Park	31	Queen's Wood & Highgate Wood
13	Horniman Museum	32	Hampstead Heath
14	Sydenham Hill Wood	33	Big Wood
15	Crystal Palace Park	34	Coldfall Wood
16	South Norwood Country Park	35	William Girling Reservoir
17	Beddington Farmlands	36	River Lee Country Park
18	Morden Hall Park	37	King George V Reservoirs
19	Battersea Park	38	Walthamstow Wetlands

HOW TO BIRDWATCH

EYES AND EARS

The two most important pieces of equipment you'll need are your eyes and ears.

My ears are constantly listening for new sounds to identify - despite looking at and listening to birds for nearly 40 years, I'm still learning. Birds don't read books, so don't know how they're supposed to look or sound: sometimes they will sing their song all the way through, another time only half of it. I twist my head to listen from different angles, to get a better idea of where the sound it is coming from. Use your phone to record it. The wonderful website *www.xeno-canto.org* has a Mystery Bird section where experts will hopefully tell you what it is.

With my eyes I search for movement. I'll scan nearby bushes, the horizon, the edges of lakes, the sky. . . Remember, most birds are not at your feet, so don't look down so much!

OPTICS

The minimum you need is a pair of binoculars. They should be comfortable to wear and hold, so I use 8 x 30 or 8 x 40. The first number relates to the magnification, the second to the width of the glass element (the bottom bit of the binoculars). Don't go too high with the magnification as it'll also magnify the tremor of your hands! The last number relates to how much light is let in, and how wide a view you get. The higher the better: this becomes important on overcast days, and at the beginning or end of the day.

You can throw loads of money at binoculars to get higher-quality glass to improve the quality of the

image you are looking at. But the main thing is to buy from an established shop. You don't even need to buy brand-new, as several shops sell second-hand pairs.

The final things are the strap – invest in a good wide one to spread the weight – and a rainguard, to protect them from the rain (and any food you may consume while you're out).

LAST THINGS

I would always recommend carrying a notebook, so you can write down what you've seen and make a note of birds you couldn't identify. You can also use apps – I use the British Trust for Ornithology's BirdTrack. Entering your records on BirdTrack will allow the BTO to look at trends on a national scale, so you are giving something back to conservation.

Finally, clothing: for me, comfort is everything,

and I try to stay as cool, dry and warm as possible. It doesn't always work, so I do get the odd boot full of water!

BIRDS IN YOUR GARDEN

A great way to attract birds just outside your kitchen window is to hang up a bird feeder – reserves like Rainham and the London Wetland Centre sell an amazing range of gourmet bird cuisine: mixed seeds, peanuts, fat balls. . . Different food will attract different species: nijer seeds goldfinches; peanuts woodpeckers. In London, however, you may find grey squirrels a problem, but you can buy specialised 'Squirrel-Buster' feeders (they're a bit more expensive) that will keep them from demolishing all that expensive bird food.

BIRD WALKS

You'll find there are lots of guided bird walks you can join, at local parks or at the bigger reserves, where experts like me will point out the birds and explain what they are. They're very sociable occasions in themselves, and a great way to be introduced to lots of new species and ways of identifying them.

Above: Birdwatchers in Victoria Park.

Below: Old meets new: House Sparrow feeds alongside Ring-necked Parakeets.

WOODBERRY WETLANDS

London Wildlife Trust's beautiful new reserve in Stoke Newington

Back in the 1980s I'd be balanced on top of my Claud Butler racing bike propped up against the fence, trying to peer over. There was no public access to what was then the eastern of the two Stoke Newington Reservoirs, only viewable at all from Lordship Road, which separated it from its western twin. And that was the case all the way from 1833, when the reservoirs were constructed, to 2016, when the London Wildlife Trust, who now manage the site, opened it as a picturesque and tranquil nature reserve amidst the bustle of north London. Now you can even walk all the way round!

The east reservoir has been partly filled with reeds, an island has been created, tern rafts floated, and there's a nice café. It is amazing when you think back to the bland grass banks and hard concrete edges there used to be. All this verdant re-wilding has been funded by a large Heritage Lottery Fund grant in conjunction with Thames Water, the GLA and Berkeley Homes, who built the new estate of flats next door. This seems to have opened the eyes of property developers to what a good idea it is to help create wildlife refuges in the capital. Birds get new habitat; residents get a lovely view from their balcony.

In the summer the reeds are alive with Reed Warblers packing into every corner to breed, as do a few pairs of Reed Buntings. Cetti's Warblers sing throughout the year – a feeding station might encourage them to show more – and in 2015 they bred. In winter these reeds are great for Water Rail. The odd Bittern has also turned up.

The various pools and reed edges provide great feeding and cover for various species: in the winter Snipe can be picked out, Teal too, though Kingfishers are surprisingly just a winter visitor despite so many breeding sites nearby. Little Egrets are already coming here in the summer, and favour the north inlet at the west end, as they breed just up the road at Walthamstow Wetlands.

Nowadays you'll find breeding Tufted Duck and summering Pochards and Gadwall. Little and Great Crested Grebes both breed here with limited success, depending on the water levels: having your legs at the back doesn't help if you need to climb up to your nest in the morning! Shelduck are present in the winter and stay into the spring, but haven't bred yet. Red-crested Pochards make appearances from time to time: in the 1990s this used to be a really good wintering site for them, but I'm showing my age again!

As is typical across London, the two commonest raptors here are Peregrine and Sparrowhawk, with the surrounding tower blocks providing great perches for the former. Buzzards and Red Kites make more appearances in the summer, and now that Kestrels no longer breed here, they've become the rarest of the raptors.

Regular birds throughout the year include Green and Great Spotted Woodpeckers, four species of tit and several species of thrush. In summer warblers flock in, with Blackcaps and Chiffchaff and the odd Sedge Warbler and Whitethroat every now and then. Jays can be found around the wooded edges of the site all year. Lesser Black-backed Gulls breed on the tern rafts.

During the summer the odd wader appears, again depending on the water levels, with Common Sandpiper and Little Ringed Plover the most common. With all this water Grey Wagtails breed – up to four pairs – and also attracted to the water, or at least the airborne insect food above it, are Swifts, whose numbers can exceed a hundred at time. The local House Martin colony is for the moment no more, so this is an infrequent visitor.

Above: The chocolate brown Cetti's Warbler can be heard singing throughout the year.

Opposite left: These new reedbeds are great for Water Rail.

Opposite right: Little Egrets are already coming to Woodberry during the summer.

Left: Little Ringed Plover appear at Woodberry during summer.

Above: An aerial view of Woodberry Wetlands.

Opposite: A male Shelduck, one of our biggest ducks, and unmistakeable with its black-and-white plumage and bright red bill.

Lordship Rd
New River Path
Woodberry Down
London N16 5HQ

9 a.m. – 4.30 p.m. daily
info@woodberrywetlands.org.uk
020 3897 6154

Refreshments: Café in reserve
Toilets: in reserve

Manor House (Piccadilly Line) 10
minutes

Regular migrants include autumn Spotted Flycatchers and winter Redwings – the northern slopes of nearby Finsbury Park often hold large flocks, and they certainly move between the two sites.

Woodberry Wetlands is still a fledgling reserve, and it'll be fascinating to see over the coming years what new birds are attracted to this re-wilded landscape. But already even the bird feeders have been attracting Lesser Redpolls alongside the Reed Buntings and finches. . . One spring a Golden Oriole graced this east reservoir, and back in the 1970s it was known as a site for Smew – wouldn't it be great if they returned to Stoke Newington in winter?

WATERWORKS NATURE RESERVE

A small but delightful new reserve in the Lee Valley

The Middlesex Filter Beds, as this site was originally called, were constructed in the 1860s to provide clear water from the well to the surrounding area. One of a number of nearby leisure amenities in the Lee Valley Park that runs for miles along the River Lea in north-east London (there's also a riding centre and an ice rink), the Filter Beds were converted into a nature reserve recently and, with the addition of a café, now provide a nice short outing.

You cross over the flood channel into the reserve by means of the footbridge – depending on the level of the water it's possible to see Little Egrets here. The areas of scrub, woodlands and grassland you come to provide ideal breeding and feeding habitat for many species, so look out for Robins, Dunnocks and Blackbirds here, and listen for Song Thrushes. It's also a fabulous place for Blue, Great and Long-tailed Tits, who in the winter will flock up like buses. You can also encounter Green and Great Spotted Woodpeckers.

Follow the path all the way until it turns sharply right to the old filter beds. Here there are screens from which to watch behind so as not to disturb the birds – you can open the wooden slats to see out across the water. Everything is very close, so slowly does it.

Typical waterbirds present from winter onwards will include Moorhens, Coots, Teal and Little Grebes, sometimes joined by Gadwall and Shoveler. Above you Cormorants move back and forth along the river Lea or cut across heading to the Thames. From March onwards the skies above host Sand Martins.

As summer approaches the reedbeds will harbour Reed Warblers, and Reed Buntings also breed. The summer months themselves bring more warblers, with Blackcap, Chiffchaff and Whitethroat breeding.

Waterworks has produced some rare birds – mostly recently a Hoopoe. Though very small compared some of the other reserves in London, for an hour or two's wander it's a little pot of gold.

Above left: Sand Martins hawk the skies for insects from April onwards.

Above right: The Dunnock, or Hedge Sparrow, is actually an accentor, and identifiable by its slate-grey head.

Opposite above: A Little Grebe on one of the lakes at Waterworks.

Opposite below: The bridge leading to the reserve.

VISITOR INFORMATION
Lammas Road (off Lea Bridge Road)
Leyton
London E10 7QB

8 a.m.–4 p.m. daily
020 8988 7566
waterworks@leevalleypark.org.uk

Refreshments: café in reserve
Toilets: in reserve

Lea Bridge (National Rail), 10 minutes

WANSTEAD PARK & FLATS

Flat, yes, but always birds to see

On London's eastern fringe you'll come to the southern edge of Epping Forest, which is Wanstead Park and Flats. Don't be expecting ancient woodland, however: it isn't that wooded. Indeed, Wanstead Flats, situated just north of Forest Gate, is, as the name suggests, a very open area with a few ponds. The stand-out record for the site is probably the singing Blyth's Reed Warbler, for just one day in May 2014!

Since both sites are next to one another you can explore them together, but they can just as well be visited separately: with different habitats they offer their own special species. If you want a circular walk, then from Wanstead Park cut down Wanstead Park Avenue to bring you back to Wanstead Flats.

At the east end of Wanstead Flats is Alexandra Lake; on the west side is Jubilee Pond: these are the ones to focus on. Your typical spread of Coots, Moorhens, Mallards and feral geese is augmented during the winter by a few Pochards, Tufted Duck, Shoveler and Gadwall – not in record-breaking numbers, but then we're not here just for wildfowl. This is also a great area for gulls, with Common Gulls very dominant, and as many as 800 being recorded! In the late summer from July the odd Yellow-legged Gull appears among the hordes.

In summer there are still a few pairs of Skylarks and Meadow Pipits left but without fenced-off areas to protect them they suffer lots of disturbance. Summer is a great time to visit, however, as the low scrub provides an excellent breeding habitat for Whitethroats, Dunnocks and Blackcaps, who all do very well here. It is possible to see Green and Great Spotted Woodpeckers on the Flats, but their numbers are higher in Wanstead Park as it is more wooded.

For the spring and autumn migration keep your eyes peeled for Wheatears and Whinchats, which can reach double figures. This is also a great place for Spotted Flycatchers and Redstarts – the autumn from August to September is best. Tree Pipits are a

regular migrant, and recently Wrynecks, a most unusual bird for Greater London, have been making an appearance, but are not annual. Once the migration explodes in October and thrushes are on the move then around mid-October the odd Ring Ouzel is found. Stonechats move through too as expected, and every now and then a bird or two stays for the winter. Linnet winter in the area too, and a few stick around during the breeding season.

In the north-west corner of the Flats is the main wood, Bush Wood, where most woodland species can be encountered. It's here you'll connect with Nuthatches, and it's good for Treecreepers, too, as well as a wintering hot spot for Firecrest.

Most large open spaces in London now have large flocks of Carrion Crows. The flats do too, but joining the ranks are the smarter and more cute Jackdaws. Large flocks of Starlings charge about on the short grass, and Pied Wagtails are also present. Grey Wagtails make the odd visit to the stretches of water.

Now for Wanstead Park. This borders a golf course to the north and the river Roding to the east. At the west end is the Wood Reservoir – Tawny Owls here – and just east of the wood is Shoulder of Mutton Pond, which is great for Reed Warbler and Water Rails in the winter: the earlier the better for seeing the latter.

We then run straight into Heronry Pond, which doesn't have a heronry on it any more. This is good for Kingfishers, however, and when I was shown around we had great views of one. Little Egrets are often present too. More of your typical wildfowl frequent these two ponds from time to time.

One more lake, this time Perch Lake – I have no idea if it has any Perch in it, but I hope so – which hosts Great Crested Grebe and is another good place for Water Rail. The whole of this area is more wooded, and so during the winter months the trees can hold Siskin. In the spring we are knee-deep in Blackcaps and Chiffchaffs.

After passing the Old Sewage farm we reach the River Roding, where Bullfinches make appearances. The river is great too for Kingfisher and Little Egret, and now Cetti's Warblers have arrived as well.

VISITOR INFORMATION
Always open

020 8532 1010

Refreshments: café in Wanstead Park
Toilets: in Wanstead Park

Leytonstone, Wanstead or Redbridge (Central Line); Wanstead Park (Overground); Manor Park (National Rail)

Opposite: The Wryneck (so-called for its unique habit of turning its head a full 180 degrees) is a rare and notable visitor at Wanstead Flats.

Right: A Moorhen at Wanstead. Smaller than a Coot, with its distinctive multi-coloured bill.

Above: Male Pochards are unmistakable with their bright chestnut head, grey, finely barred body and black rear.

Left: Great Spotted Woodpecker can be seen at Wanstead.

Opposite: Kew Gardens is playing host to this Ring-necked Parakeet.

Landmark London Birds: **PARAKEET**

Nearly every park in the capital now has these iconic bright–green, long– tailed, non–natives birds. Where did they come from?

Rumours persist that they escaped from the set of The *African Queen* at Shepperton Studios, or were released by Jimi Hendrix when he was living in Mayfair. Neither is true: they probably escaped from someone's cage-bird collection.

The first published records of Ring-necked Parakeets in London start in 1970. I first ventured off to see them at Chiswick House in the 1980s, a posh bit of town: by then up to a hundred were being seen together, spread over fewer than 20 different sites in a small section of West London.

In the mid-1990s counts breached the 1,000 mark, and by the early 2000s had reached 7,000: the population was on the move. They had headed east, hitting Hampstead Heath, and at the same time taken a more southerly route, to penetrate South London. Eventually numbers exceeded 20,000 birds – and from just three winter roost sites. Parakeets are now in every corner of the capital.

The species is communal-roosting, so large groups gather together in small areas to sleep for the night. In the breeding season the males apparently leave the females on the nest and continue to roost with all their mates!

Native to India and some parts of Africa, Ring-necked Parakeets are known to cause damage to crops – currently the main problem with this species. They can also damage trees by stripping off the growing buds. Also, they're thought to take over woodpeckers' nests, and a recent study in Spain revealed they're attacking bats and evicting them from their nests. Parakeets may be nice to look at, but we need to keep an eye on them.

FAIRLOP WATERS COUNTRY PARK

Flooded gravel pits at the eastern end of the Central Line

Most lakes in the London area, apart from those in formally landscaped parks, were created by gravel extraction – indeed, here at Fairlop it is still carried on nearby. Here, at the far eastern reaches of the Central Line (this is where those trains for 'Hainault via Newbury Park' go), we are again right on the boundary between the city and the countryside: leave the Tube station and almost immediately you're walking with farmland beside you.

Fairlop Waters Country Park caters for several outdoor pursuits: there is a sailing club, a golfing range, as well as a bar/restaurant, and don't forget the dog walkers and anglers. It can get busy here. Despite all this activity birds are a real draw: I still recall coming once to see a Great Northern Diver feeding on the main lake. Amazingly, a Razorbill was found too, and a Long-tailed Duck. Normally you'd have to go all the way to somewhere like Dungeness in Kent to stand even a chance of seeing birds like that.

Besides the main lake there are two more stretches of water here: the fishing lake on the east side, and the lagoon pit to the south. All three attract wildfowl, including Teal, Gadwall, Shoveler and Great Crested Grebe. Joining them are Grey Herons, Cormorants and, more recently, Little Egrets.

This area still holds a wintering flock of Lapwing, which commute between the island on the main lake and farmland to the east, their square, flappy wings flickering black-white, black-white against the sky. In the late 1980s it numbered over a thousand birds, but their subsequent decline mirrors a wider impact on their population across the UK, largely down to the ever more aggressive management of arable farmland. Small numbers of Golden Plover are also present – another species one doesn't think of anywhere near a city.

A large section of scrub along the south-east corner of the site and a wooded section directly south of the main lake provide

Above: A Lapwing at Fairlop, distinguished in flight by the bold black-and-white wing pattern.

Opposite: Canada Geese in profusion on the lake at Fairlop.

excellent breeding habitat for Blackcaps, Chiffchaff, Whitethroat and smaller numbers of Willow Warblers. In the winter this ground becomes flooded and holds Snipe and the odd Woodcock too. Occasional waders turn up on migration, including Common and Green Sandpipers.

Just south of here the stable paddocks, accessed via a public bridleway, feature fences and hedgerows good for migrants in the early autumn: look for Lesser Whitethroat, Redstart, Spotted Flycatcher, Whinchat, and even Black Redstart, Ring Ouzel and Tree Pipit. Redwings and Fieldfare can appear anywhere as they migrate through. Little Owls are regular in the paddock area. The usual raptors can be seen, but there's the possibility of encountering Red Kite and Hobby too.

Rare birds seen at Fairlop Waters don't just include the oddities on the lake, but also Hoopoe, Red-backed Shrike, and once, would you believe, a magnificent Hume's Yellow-browed Warbler for a few months.

VISITOR INFORMATION
Fairlop Waters
Forest Road
Barkingside
Essex
IG6 3HN

020 8500 9911
fairlopwaters@vision-rcl.org.uk

7.00 a.m. – 11.00 p.m., Monday–Thursday
7.00 a.m. – midnight, Friday & Saturday
7.00 a.m. – 10.30 p.m., Sunday

Refreshments: bar and restaurant in park
Toilets: in park

Fairlop (Central Line), 10 minutes

Opposite top: A flock of Golden Plover in flight above Fairlop Waters.

VICTORIA PARK

Sparrowhawks and woodpeckers breeding in a big local park

This sumptuous park in east London, designed by James Pennethorne as the sister park to Battersea Park, was laid out after a petition to Queen Victoria urging her to help improve the health of people in the East End. Though huge – a mile from end to end - it is still very much a local park and, while it hasn't produced anything startlingly rare, with lots of mature trees and three lakes it does attract a lot of birds. Earlier in the morning is best; at the eastern end there is a lot of sporting activity, while hot days will inevitably bring sun-worshippers out.

The bigger west lake (where the café sits on the shore) has the most wildfowl. Here you'll usually encounter Great Crested and Little Grebes, who like the areas of overhanging vegetation on the east side and north of Pagoda Island (the building of the Pagoda has not helped the fortunes of the herons on it). Tufted Duck, Coot and Moorhen are always present, as are feral Canada, Greylag and the striking apricot-hued Egyptian Geese (these in low numbers).

The globally threatened Common Pochards breed here, as do the feral Red-crested Pochards with their punky scarlet crests – you can see anything from a few to a dozen. The publisher of this book, who used to live next to Victoria Park, proudly tells me he once saw a Pintail on this lake.

Overhead, Cormorants commute from their main breeding site at Walthamstow Reservoir; look for them also around the edges of the islands, resting with their wings hanging out. Kingfishers do make appearances, as well as along the Regent's Canal where it borders

the park's southern rim, but, because they have become so tolerant of people they don't fly or call much, and are consequently difficult to locate.

The east lake is better. During the summer months a bit of rain brings insects low over the lakes, and Swifts and Sand Martins whizz down to feed on them.

North of the west lake is a patch of trees and bushes called the Grove, good for warblers including Goldcrests, which like the evergreens, and the occasional Firecrest winters here. Blackcaps can be heard in the bushes and breed in the park.

Above: A Sparrowhawk, hard to see as its speeds through the trees hunting. In the second half of the winter they can be seen displaying, as they fly straight up and then suddenly drop down.

Victoria Park
Grove Road
Bow
London E3 5TB

7 a.m. – dusk, all year round

parks@towerhamlets.gov.uk

Refreshments: two cafés in park
Toilets: in park

Cambridge Heath and Hackney Wick
(Overground), 10 minutes; Bethnal
Green (Central Line), 15 minutes

Opposite top left: Kingfishers can appear by the lakes in Victoria Park.

Opposite top right: A Coot on a nest. It will build it with twigs and vegetation, plus various discarded rubbish, including the dreaded plastic bag!

Right: A juvenile Cuckoo with its barred plumage. Cuckoos are confusable with Sparrowhawks, which however lack the barring on their backs.

From August, tit flocks build up and can even reach a few hundred; Willow Warblers and Chiffchaffs will often be among them.

Sparrowhawks breed here – early in the year you'll see them displaying and frequently above the well-used footpaths. One year they nested next door to the Lovebox music festival! The young fledged, too. Several pairs of Mistle Thrushes breed and can be seen throughout the year. All the open spaces of grass are worth a scan for these bold thrushes: listen out for their rattling call as they bounce through the sky in their undulating flight.

Great Spotted Woodpeckers breed, as do several pairs of Stock Doves in the park, the latter gliding around on their display flights in the spring. Winter months will always turn up some northern thrushes, perhaps a dozen Redwings or Fieldfares bounding about on the grass or plunging into the berry-infested bushes.

For the last three years I have been leading birding walks around Victoria Park, and it's amazing what turns up: Cuckoo, Common Sandpiper, Rook and Spotted Flycatcher – none amazingly rare in themselves, but excellent birds to see amid such an urban environment.

TOWER HAMLETS CEMETERY

Woodland birds among the Victorian dead

Despite the hustle and bustle of the city you can still find some lovely pockets of proper wilderness, like this cemetery. Tower Hamlets Cemetery Park was one of the seven cemeteries created for the growing capital by the Victorians – others include the equally remarkable ones at Nunhead, Highgate and Abney Park in Stoke Newington.

In 1966 it ceased to be used as a cemetery, and was later given park status by an Act of Parliament. Over more than a century its grand, often huge, tombstones, monuments and mausoleums have become coated in moss and lichen, some now leaning at an angle half-buried in vegetation. These days a wide variety of activities can be enjoyed here: one year I led a birding walk and came upon a group of artists drawing a naked model – not what I was expecting to show the group.

It is a rich wood and, even with many people visiting it, still very attractive to wildlife. The most noteworthy species to be found is Firecrest, which has wintered here on a regular basis since at least 2008. Most years two birds or more turn up and stay through to the beginning of the spring, often breaking into song. They tend to favour the patch of ivy-clad trees on the west side called Sanctuary Wood.

Goldcrest are also here in winter, so the cemetery is not just a Firecrest haven. Winter is also good for Redwings, and the odd Fieldfare makes an appearance although the site is not really suited to the species.

Summer brings a nice collection of birds, with several woodland species like Great Spotted Woodpecker, Jay and Stock Dove. The majority should be relatively straightforward to pick up either by sight or vocally. Since the cemetery is full of small birds such as Great and Blue Tits, Sparrowhawks breed here, and can be found hunting through the rides.

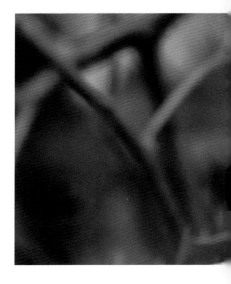

Above: A tiny Firecrest, distinguished from the similar Goldcrest by its white stripe over the eye and bronze shoulder patch.

Right: Snowdrops adorn the old cemetery in early spring.

VISITOR INFORMATION
Southern Grove
London E3

dawn – dusk, all year round
0208 9836 1277
contact@fothcp.org, parks@towerhamlets.gov.uk

Toilets: Soanes Centre near entrance

Mile End (Central, District and Hammersmith &
City Lines), 5 minutes

Blackcaps are widespread, with up to a half dozen pairs breeding, Chiffchaffs breed in summer too, though only a couple of pairs, and odd birds do turn up in the winter too. This kind of habitat is hard to visit without seeing or hearing the hordes of Blackbirds, Wrens and Robins which form the bulk of the breeding population. The widespread and larger-than-life Wood Pigeons on display flights, wing-clapping overhead during the summer, are always an enjoyable experience.

Left: A Wren, with its characteristically cocked tail.

Opposite: Kingfishers, much like certain cans of lager, reach the parts of London other birds can't reach, like this one on the River Wandle near Colliers Wood.

London is full of water, from local rivers and small ponds in local parks to the massive River Thames and gigantic reservoirs. These all contain fish, and predators come to feed on them. One of the best-looking is the Kingfisher.

These gorgeous-looking little birds will perch motionless, waiting for an unsuspecting fish to appear, before diving in head first for their prey. They like overhanging perches to fish from – typically bushes, but here in the capital a discarded shopping trolley does the trick just as well.

Perhaps the easiest way to find one is too learn their call, a short, sharp, loud 'zii' often repeated, especially early in the breeding season when pairs will chase each other up and down calling frantically. Otherwise, look for a small darting blue torpedo charging across the water.

So check your local river, stream, lake, pond or reservoir, and even the shore of the Thames. I once saw one in front of Tate Modern – I only noticed it when a Peregrine suddenly dived at the shore, flushing it up, predictably without success.

HORNCHURCH COUNTRY PARK & INGREBOURNE HILL

Yellowhammers and Bramblings at this new reserve in the east

Here, on the very eastern edge of London, where the urban environment meets some rather sprawling countryside, is a new reserve managed by Havering Council, on the site of the historic Hornchurch aerodrome – a famous Battle of Britain Aerodrome during the war. It only opened in 2015 and is a great place to visit.

The visitor centre, called the Ingrebourne Valley Vistor Centre, managed by the Essex Wildlife Trust, is well equipped, with feeders in front of it and a noticeboard of recent sightings, and is a great place from which to view the River Ingrebourne cutting through its valley. Gone are the days of an old wooden hut with a few leaflets (perhaps I'm showing my age, as my birding life now spans four decades!): today's self-respecting reserves will have palatial information centres with cafés and clean toilets. Guided walks around the reserve are available – check out the EWT website.

This is a very simple site to navigate: just walk straight south from the centre to the viewing point. Here in the winter you can pick up Teal feeding in front of you, who don't seem to care about the sometimes large numbers of people wandering by.

Expect to see Shoveler, Gadwall, the elusive Snipe and an occasional Green Sandpiper – indeed, these species may be on any of the bodies of water from here down to Ingrebourne Hill (managed by the Forestry Commission). Water Rails are present throughout the year, but you might not know, given their ability to stay out of sight. Check with the visitor

Left: The striking Yellowhammer is increasingly uncommon these days, but is clinging on at Hornchurch.

Opposite above: Bramblings are another great bird to see in Greater London, sometimes present in winter flocks on Hornchurch's farmland.

Opposite below: A beautiful male Bullfinch with its salmon-pink chest.

centre for any spots the odd more ostentatious bird may be frequenting.

Hornchurch Country Park is possibly where the East London population of Cetti's Warbler originated from: back in the early 2000s its numbers here exploded, and spread into the neighbouring Rainham Marshes. Now they seem to be every dozen or so metres, and their very loud song is nearly constant during the spring. They do sing throughout the year – just less in winter.

All the lovely vegetation here, from the wetland areas to the drier scrub, is a magnet for migrant warblers: Reed and Sedge Warbler prefer the wet habitat; Whitethroat, Lesser Whitethroat, Blackcap and even Garden Warbler are breeding in the bushes. Cuckoos are just about holding on, and can be heard during the early part of the spring. Blackbirds and Song Thrush breed, and during the winter both Redwing and Fieldfare can be seen, but note that their numbers vary from year to year.

Just beyond the viewpoint a path cuts off to your left, heading east over the farmland. This is a good track to follow to pick up the reduced population of Yellowhammers, a much-threatened bird in Britain that is clinging on here. This farmland is very good for finches in the winter, and can hold Bramblings, which are sometimes seen in larger flocks. Also present in the area are Pheasants and Red-legged Partridge.

Head back west to the main path and follow that south again through all the scrubland and trees. This is normally a great spot for Bullfinches, a species rapidly disappearing from London, so listen out for their soft calls. Grey Herons breed in the tall trees, but viewing them is difficult.

Beyond here the ground opens up, and you'll see a large hill in front of you. This is the Ingrebourne Hill:

VISITOR INFORMATION
Ingrebourne Valley Visitor Centre
Hornchurch Country Park
Squadrons Approach
Hornchurch
RM12 6DF

9 a.m. – 5 p.m. daily (– 4 p.m. November – January)
Closed: Christmas Day and Boxing Day

01708 520364

ingrebourne@essexwt.org.uk

Refreshments: café in visitor centre
Toilets: in visitor centre

Elm Park or Hornchurch (District Line)

head straight over it, and as you go you'll be hitting the breeding grounds for Skylarks and Meadow Pipits. Both are present during winter too, but generally keep low, and are not up in the sky singing away as they do from the spring through the summer months. It can be a good area for Wheatear and Whinchat, too, but less so when it is busy with people. Just south of here is another pool which also holds wildfowl and, if you haven't yet seen a Great Crested Grebe, Tufted Duck or Pochard, stop for a close look.

With all this wild open space raptors are well represented. Kestrel, Sparrowhawk and Buzzard all breed, and Barn Owls and Marsh Harriers make the odd appearance. In the summer all the stretches of water are rich with dragonflies and damselflies, which pull in Hobbys, who can reach up to a dozen birds at the same time!

Left: Red-legged Partridge can also be found on the farmland.

Opposite: A Peregrine Falcon flying past St Paul's Cathedral.

In the late 1970s when I started birdwatching, Peregrines were primarily a west-coast bird – my first was on the Pembrokeshire coast. It appeared from nowhere, and within seconds was a dot far out to sea!

It was years before my first one in London, on the South Bank in the early 1990s: an immature bird drifted around and disappeared behind what would become Tate Modern. I never thought to check the tower for birds roosting. Later that year they were discovered there.

Over the next ten years I watched them there regularly: up to five different individuals, but they didn't breed. They had been breeding in New York for many years: now they were becoming a London species!

During the next decade more pairs started appearing across the capital, and breeding began at the turn of century. They were replacing their native cliff-face nests with London's concrete towers. Rural Peregrines don't nest close to one another, but their urban cousins are breeding less than a mile apart, principally at the old buildings along the Thames.

Nest boxes have significantly improved their breeding success, as they are no longer affected by high winds or heavy rainfall, and at various sites cameras now let you watch them online. These have proved very informative on the ecology of these masterful hunters: while the majority of their feeding happens in the first and last hour of daylight, nocturnal feeding has been confirmed. The capital's ambient light lights up the streams of birds migrating at night, enabling Peregrines to feed on them.

The population is booming, with over thirty pairs breeding in the capital. It always pays to look up at tall buildings: if the odd feather drops down, look out – a Peregrine may be consuming its latest meal.

RAINHAM MARSHES

The RSPB's flagship nature reserve at the edge of Greater London

On the far eastern fringe of Greater London, adjoining the northern bank of the Thames, lies the vast expanse of Rainham Marshes.

Over the years these marshes found use as a firing range for the MoD, a rubbish tip, and a dumping ground for silt dredged from the bottom of the Thames. Nowadays, all these strange activities have given way to wildlife conservation: as the RSPB's flagship nature reserve in London it is one of the very best places to watch birds around the capital. Opened in 2006, it already boasts a long list of amazing species and, despite being bounded by the A13 dual carriageway and Eurostars swishing across the Channel Tunnel railway viaduct, retains a real atmosphere of remoteness. Over 100 species have been recorded in one day; I led a group around in autumn and managed more than 80.

Rainham Marshes can consume a whole day's birding or just a few hours' fresh air and wilderness action with the family. We'll cover the RSPB section first, where the full circular walk is about 2.5 miles, but you can do it all in one hit via public transport, starting at Rainham Station and finishing at Purfleet Station (the closest to the reserve).

During the winter the five main stretches of water heave with wildfowl and wader: expect lots of Wigeon, with Teal, Shoveler and Gadwall also in good numbers, and often a few Pintail. Lapwings can run to a thousand, with Golden Plover sometimes present.

From July onwards Black-tailed Godwits appear, while Redshank in their spotty summer plumage sit on fence posts on the look-out for trouble. I've even managed to find a few groups of Temmincks' Stint. Over the last few years Bitterns have been making appearances, but you'll need to be very fortunate to see one.

The shoreline of the river is very good for Rock Pipits, and a regular spot for Water Pipits, with several birds moving from their mountainous breeding ranges to spend the winter along the Thames. This is the favoured area for Shelduck, displaying, chasing and calling from spring onwards. Look across to the far bank of the river: at low tide there may well be several seals flopped up on the mud.

Perhaps most remarkable of all, for the last few years Avocets have been wintering locally, and at low tide 20 or so can be seen on the foreshore right next to the reserve. Difficult to believe that only a few decades ago you had to travel to Suffolk to see the RSPB's beautiful logo-bird.

Opposite top: With the Channel Tunnel rail viaduct beyond, the scrape teems with Wigeon and Coot.

Opposite bottom left: A small population of beautiful Bearded Tits can be found by their 'pinging' call.

Opposite bottom right: Marsh Harriers are a regular fixture at Rainham. Several can be seen in one day drifting low over the vegetation.

Rainham is excellent for warblers, with most vegetation near water seeming to hold Sedge or Reed Warbler, and male Whitethroats exploding into song in spring and dancing through the sky displaying for a mate. The bushes around the Cordite Store – another fascinating relic of the firing range - hold Blackcaps, Chiffchaffs and the odd secretive Lesser Whitethroat. Cetti's Warblers' improbably loud, rusty-hinge singing is heard throughout the year - amazing to think they only arrived here in the last ten years or so.

Another feather in Rainham's cap is its small numbers of beautiful Bearded Tits breeding. Currently they favour the Dragonfly Pool area: listen out for their 'pinging' calls. Kingfishers have bred in front of the Marshland Discovery Hide, and if you are willing to wait you can watch them feeding their young.

Rainham used to be the epicentre for Hen Harriers in London, but numbers have been decimated by illegal persecution elsewhere. But Marsh Harriers quarter the site year-round, wafting above the reedbeds, while Peregrines, Sparrowhawks and Kestrels frequent the electricity pylons. In the summer Hobbys are frequent visitors, gorging on the abundant dragonflies. Barn Owls are resident – check in the visitor centre which nestbox they are favouring.

If gulls are your thing then Rainham has a long list. From July onwards Yellow-legged Gulls can exceed over a hundred birds, joined by the odd Caspian Gull and sometimes, following boats up the river in winter, Kittiwakes. Lovely 'winter-wingers' – Iceland and Glaucous Gulls – feed on the mud along the shoreline and float on the Thames.

From the start of spring Rainham is a great place to witness bird migration: not just warblers but Yellow Wagtails, which used to breed here in large numbers, Whinchats and Wheatears, Spotted Flycatchers and Redstarts in the bushes, and even a Ring Ouzel or three. By late spring Swifts can gather here into their thousands. This whole area also holds the London record for Wood Pigeon migration, at over 50,000 in a morning!

From the visitor centre the riverside path leads west beyond the reserve alongside the large grassy hill that is the former landfill

Above: Whitethroats are a common fixture at Rainham, and their numbers swell from late April.

Opposite top: From the path that leads up onto the top of the former landfill site you scan for Skylarks, Meadow Pipits and raptors.

Opposite left: Short-eared Owls make appearances at Rainham and sometimes linger into the spring.

Opposite right: A Snipe at Rainham with its disproportionately long bill.

Above: The Stone Barges (actually made from concrete) are the remains of one of the unused Mulberry Harbours construction for the D-Day Landings in 1944. Favoured by Water Pipits, here they are used by waders to roost on at high tide. Black-tailed Godwit are the dominant species, with some Redshank and Dunlin.

Left: These old shooting targets are a relic of the reserve's past as an MoD firing range.

Opposite: The RSPB's striking visitor centre has a café, toilets, binoculars for hire, and regular guided walks. House sparrows and finches descend in numbers on the feeders outside.

VISITOR INFORMATION
RSPB Rainham Marshes
New Tank Hill Rd
Purfleet
Essex
RM19 1SZ

9.30 a.m. – 5 p.m. daily February –
October; 9.30 a.m. – 4.30 p.m.
November–January
Closed on Christmas Day and
Boxing Day

01708 899840
rainham.marshes@rspb.org.uk

Purfleet (National Rail), 20 mins

Admission fee for non-RSPB-
members

site – now mostly capped, but still with a small working section –
and the path running over the top gives amazing views across the
reserve and river. During spring and summer the heavens are filled
with parachuting Meadow Pipits and Skylarks ascending ever
higher, singing continuously. This is a good spot for the odd pair
of breeding Stonechats, and Ravens cronking through the sky.
Here, and the Serin Mound just to the north (named after the
Serins that once wintered here, though they don't now), is a
good vantage-point for scanning for raptors.

Further west along the shore, the Stone Barges, a strange,
watery Stonehenge, are a landmark in their own right, and
favourites of Water Pipits, who like to stand on them at high tide.
Due north, silt from the Thames was still being pumped into the
Silt Lagoons as recently as the 1980s: in the summer you could find
a large group of Little Ringed Plovers on the mud. Finally you come
to West Rainham Marsh, a network of ditches, reeds, scrub and
cattle grazing, good for returning Cuckoos, and alive in the summer
with the continuous reeling of Grasshopper Warblers towards the
end of the day.

SOUTHEND-ON-SEA

A day at the seaside for geese and waders

This will not be on everyone's radar. At just over 50 minutes from London by train, and with everything within walking distance, Southend-on-Sea is a typical Essex resort and an easy day or even half-day out. Beach, fish and chips, funfair, amusements – you can see why it attracts lots of visitors. And it isn't even quite at the seaside, but only near the end of the Thames Estuary. Other projected 'seaside' resorts a little further up the Thames like Canvey Island and, on the south bank, All-hallows-on-Sea, never quite took off, but Southend on a sunny summer weekend will be teeming. But it's also an amazing birdwatching site.

There are two main locations. One is the seafront itself – both east and west of the pier is good, and you don't need to walk too far to see some great birds. Since Southend is not a nature reserve you'll find very little information around the town, however, so for up-to-date news check the websites of the Southend Ornithological Group and the South-East Essex RSPB Groups.

And then there's the pier, nearly two hundred years old and, at 1.34 miles, the longest anywhere in the world. You'll arrive at the tip if you choose to reach Southend the way thousands of daytrippers used to a hundred years ago, by pleasure steamer. You can still take one today: the *Waverley*, the preserved and last sea-going paddle steamer in the world. Pick it up from the Tower of London Pier on one of its three-hour voyages downriver and end up in Southend. I did this once and had a dozen Great Skuas sitting on the water just before we got to the pier! I always walk the length of Southend Pier so as to pick up anything interesting en route, but there is a little train that runs from end to end.

Planning your trip is important, because it's very important to know when high tide is. We want to hit an incoming tide about an hour before high tide, because at low tide you'll have over a mile of mud in front of you, which means with the vast spread of food

Above: A Curlew on the mud at Southend: only the Whimbrel - a summer visitor with a seven-striped head - has a similar long, down-curved bill.

Opposite left: Southend is an easy place to see Dark-bellied Brent Geese.

Opposite right: A Redshank showing off its lovely bright, almost glowing red legs. Shank means leg.

available the birds are spread far and wide.

Southend-on-Sea offers birdwatchers three special treats. The first is Dark-bellied Brent Geese, smaller and dumpier and a great deal rarer than the ubiquitous Canada Geese. They return from their breeding grounds in the arctic tundra in late September and depart in March, but odd birds do summer in the Thames Estuary.

There aren't vast numbers here like you'll find just upriver at Leigh-on-Sea in early October – where they peak at around 8,000! – but at high tide you'll see anything from a dozen to 30, and what is so special here is how close they are. They'll just bob along the seafront feeding happily as hundreds of people walk by. Normally they're just west of the pier or at its base; once the tide ebbs they will follow the shoreline in search of food and become more distant. You can see them at different tides, but at high tide the views are sensational.

The second speciality is Mediterranean Gulls. It's possible to see them throughout the year, but July to March is the peak time, with the highest numbers in late July/early August. They'll feed with other gulls all along the seafront, but east of the pier is a good spot. The end of the pier, where there is a gull loft, can attract up to 40.

Finally, Southend is a brilliant place for waders. At high tide flocks are present feeding both east and west of the pier, mostly Turnstone and Sanderling, with lower numbers of Dunlin and Ringed Plover, but great views can also be had just with binoculars of Curlew, Redshank and Oystercatcher.

The birds west of the pier sit a few metres away from the road, while to the east they stay on the natural shingle ridges. If you sit down near them, but not too close, you'll often find they'll spread out and move towards to you, offering amazing views. Once the tide's zenith has peaked they start to feed on the newly exposed mud, and this is a great time to watch the Sanderling charging back and forth following the crashing waves.

Back at the end of the pier you'll also notice the ever-present Turnstones, roosting and walking about the place. They'll come right up to you and will even pick at dog-ends, but please refrain from giving them any unsuitable food. Telescopes are helpful here, but

Opposite: An adult Mediterranean Gull - the jet black head, all white wings and blood red bill distinguish it from the more ubiquitous Black-headed Gull.

Above: A mixed flock of waders roosting on the beach at high tide. The majority of them are the ghostly-looking Sanderling.

VISITOR INFORMATION
Southend Pier
Western Esplanade
Southen-on-Sea
Essex
SS1 2EL

01702 215620
council@southend.gov.uk

Check website for pier opening
times, admission prices, tide tables
etc:

Refreshments: along promenade;
Salt Café on pier
Toilets: along Promenade; in Royal
Pavilion

Southend Central or Southend
Victoria (National Rail)

Opposite above: Watching the gulls on
Southend beach.

Opposite below: A Turnstone on the pier.

Right: Birdwatchers on the Esplanade at
Southend, enjoying the mix of waders and
gulls.

not always essential, for scanning the water for seabirds,
particularly in autumn: Gannets, maybe, Great Northern and
Red-throated Divers (divers in the winter), and sometimes, if the
wind is right, Skuas. There's even a chance of seeing the odd auk
like a Guillemot. Depending on the state of the estuary and the
availability of sprats, Kittiwakes can be seen following boats, and
if you are lucky odd birds sometimes land on the pier.

EAST INDIA DOCK BASIN

Wintering duck within sight of Canary Wharf

One of London's smallest nature reserves, this miniature site is really worth a visit, for the sweeping views up- and downriver alone. Tucked away on the north bank of the Thames just below Canary Wharf – cut through the gate next to East India DLR station – here is a historic backwater of the capital.

Next door is Trinity Buoy Wharf with London's only lighthouse (the fleet of Thames Clippers moors just beyond it), and if you follow the Thames Path westwards round to Virginia Quay – now a new apartment development – you'll come to a monument on the terrace to the Virginia Settlers, who in 1606 set sail from Blackwall aboard the *Susan Constant* under Captain John Smith to establish the first English colony in the Americas, at Jamestown in Virginia. The NFL, Disneyland, Hollywood, Donald Trump – all started here...

East India Dock was built in the early 1800s, and still being used until shortly after the war for imports of spices and cloth from the East Indies. A large tidal dock with a reedbed at the north end and several small stands of trees and bushes to the south, it's managed by the Lea Valley Park Authority. There are screens to view the birds behind, but the birds see you coming anyhow!

Nowadays the main draw is the numbers of wintering duck you can see amazingly close to central London: up to several hundred Teal, with their beautiful emerald-green-striped heads and buttermilk rumps, as well as Shelduck and Shoveler.

In the summer common terns breed on the tern raft, and will sometimes loiter on the posts around the edge of the dock providing excellent views. During the summer when the tide is out, especially April/May, Little Ringed Plovers can be found feeding on the mud. Their numbers vary year to year, and early morning is the best time to catch them. Moorhens disappear in and out of the reedbed, which holds a handful of Reed Warblers.

The small copse is the best in the area for Wrens, Robins and Blackbirds, and the dock itself can host breeding Sand Martins. Black

Redstarts breed in the area but can be difficult to track down - check any derelict industrial land. One morning here I heard a male singing continuously for three hours! Linnets, Greenfinches, Goldfinches, Grey Wagtails, Grey Herons and Little Egrets can be found anywhere around the site.

Cormorants roosting on the jetty to the west have included visitors from Estonia, the rings on their legs proving the distances birds are travelling to the capital. Gulls are of course always present, but Yellow-legged Gulls can be seen here too.

VISITOR INFORMATION

East India Dock Basin
Orchard Place
London E14 9QS

8.30 a.m. – dusk.

03000 030 610
info@leevalleypark.org.uk

East India (DLR), 5 minutes

Above: A young male Black Redstart singing at East India Dock – a haunt for them still, but they are never easy to see or hear.

Below: Two Cormorants roosting on a jetty, the right hand bird is ringed and originally from Estonia! Now spending its winters in the capital.

Opposite above: A Common Tern at East India Dock.

Opposite below: A male Teal. Perhaps the best location in the capital to see this species in winter?

GREENWICH PENINSULA ECOLOGY PARK

A tiny oasis a short flight from the O2

Opened in 2002, this magical place, hardly more than a stone's throw from the O2, shows you can create something great amid a sea of concrete, and is the kind of thing we need more of across London. At four acres it's very small, but its urban wetland attempts to restore a piece of the marshland the whole Greenwich Peninsula would originally have been. For wildlife it's pure gold, and birds are well represented.

It can be good for migrants, though like most small sites a bit hit-and-miss, and especially when lots of people visit. The Greenwich Peninsula as a whole has a long list of great records, including Red-backed Shrike and Serin, but unfortunately the loss of brownfield sites, as more and more of the post-industrial wasteland is redeveloped for housing, means Black Redstarts no longer breed here.

You reach the Ecology Park from North Greenwich Tube station, cutting through Central Park, a green space that holds Chaffinches in the winter as well as Goldfinches, which also breed locally. Though the boardwalk around the perimeter is always open, the reserve itself is currently only open from Wednesday to Sunday – please check the website for times.

As you wander in from the visitor centre, where you can check what's about (in the winter of 2017/18 a beautiful Jack Snipe was present!), you find yourself in a small wooded section, the majority of it towering Alders. These are great for birds, and are full of Goldfinch during the winter and from year to year will often yield at least a few Siskin.

Thames Path
John Harrison Way
London SE10 0QZ

Wednesday–Sunday 10 a.m. – 5 p.m.
(Spring and Summer); 10 a.m. – dusk
(Autumn and Winter); closed over
Christmas period
Outer boardwalk open 24 hours

gpep@tcv.org.uk
0208 293 1904

North Greenwich (Jubilee Line), 10
minutes

Opposite top: Siskins at the Ecology Park
favour the Alder trees.

Opposite bottom: A Jack Snipe at the Ecology
Park - smaller and shorter-billed than Snipe,
with diagnostic double stripe over the eye. This
stripe is called the supercilium.

The whole site is very wet, and the reeds hold Water Rail in the winter, small in number and hard to see or hear (though their squealing cry is unmistakeable when you do), but sometimes visible picking around the edges of the two lakes. In the summer they're replaced by Reed Warblers: once their broods fledge excellent views can be had of them stumbling through the vegetation. There are two hides to watch from.

As you can imagine, given how small the reserve is, only a handful of wildfowl are present, with Mallard, Coot and Moorhen all year round and breeding. Teal make winter appearances at high tide.

The feeders are very well used, and during my most recent winter visit Greenfinch, Goldfinch, Blue Tit, Great Tit, Long-tailed Tit and Siskin were feeding at point-blank range. Winter is boosted with migrating Redwings, and Chiffchaffs and Goldcrests, but perhaps the best winter bird is Kingfisher! Spring and summer bring breeding Common Terns – eight pairs recently – and Blackcap. Spring can be full of migrant warblers.

The Greenwich Peninsula Ecology Park is an insect heaven, and so in summer butterflies and dragonflies compete for airspace. It currently holds the only known UK population of a rare bee, *Hoplitis Adunca*! What else is out there to be discovered in our capital?

Opposite: One of London's 850,000+ feral Pigeons surveys the city it owns.

Love them or hate them, Feral Pigeons are part of our cities.

The Feral Pigeon originated from our native Rock Dove, which was originally kept to carry messages on small pieces of paper attached to its legs, and then used to race other pigeons up and down the country. But some made an exit, and realised that nesting under our bridges or on the front of buildings was just like their native cliffs on our coasts.

With numbers in London reaching 850,000 there are loads of them. Why so many? Well, they turned up before the Peregrines came in, so have few natural predators to keep them in check. Then we leave loads of food waste about, and they come and eat it. These left-over scraps are not very good for them, which is another reason why we should bin our food waste.

But London doesn't just have Feral Pigeons: we have Wood Pigeons as well, and loads of them too. They breed in most parks and gardens, and pretty much any tree or bush available.

What else? Collared Doves, who can breed throughout the year, which is part of their success. They haven't been in the country for long, starting to spread across Europe from the Middle East in the 1900s, and the first few not arriving in the UK till the 1950s. They're now one of our top ten commonest birds in the UK. That's impressive!

GREENWICH PARK

A striking Observatory for bird migration

This beautiful Royal Park holds the old Royal Observatory, through which runs the Greenwich Meridian marking longitude 0°, so you can stand in both eastern and western hemispheres at the same time. Like all the capital's major parks it's a very popular destination for tourists, families and locals, particularly in fine weather, but as a substantial tract of verdant and varied green space it's also somewhere you can see quite a lot of bird life if you look for it.

It has two levels: the lower section where the National Maritime Museum is located, very open and covered in short manicured grass, and the upper section with the Observatory on its brow. This upper plateau differs significantly, with grand veteran Sweet Chestnut trees, dense scrubland and deep holly, and is best for birds. In the enclosure at the south-east corner, to which there is no public access, a small population of Red and Fallow Deer adds more variety. Redwings passing through in winter tend to favour this deer park, and may be joined by the odd Fieldfare.

A small pond in the upper section has a captive population of Tufted Duck and Pochard, which is unexpected given how common they are as a wild species across the capital. The odd wild individual will turn up too, which means checking individual wings for signs of pinioning to make sure it's not part of the collection. One winter a small group of Teal decided they liked the lake so much they stayed the winter.

The dense cover of trees and bushes provides great habitat and is reflected in the number of species present. Look out for Nuthatches and Great Spotted Woodpeckers, and of course the ubiquitous Ring-necked Parakeets. What else? Your usual collection of Tits is boosted by Coal Tit, and among warblers Blackcaps and Chiffchaff breed, with the odd pair of Whitethroats still just about holding on. Ever-energetic Goldcrests breed here too, these tiny birds manically hopping around inside a tree's canopy, and the park

has also held several winter Firecrest. Check all the holly bushes, especially between the lake and the deer park: seeing a Firecrest always brightens the day.

Jackdaws, with their bright silver eyes, have recently returned to the area, and are now everywhere. A careful search of the trees may reveal Stock Dove: they are still relatively shy compared to their bulkier cousin the Wood Pigeon. Chaffinch numbers have increased over recent years from none to over a dozen, and a few pairs of the increasingly rare Greenfinch are still here.

From the vantage-point of the Observatory at the very top, with its amazing panoramic view across London, bird migrations can be witnessed with binoculars as flocks stream in from the continent up the line of the Thames. Well, sometimes more like trickle...

Autumn, especially October to early November, holds the longer spread and greater volume of migrants, and early mornings are best. Thrushes, finches and Wood Pigeons make up most of the migrant flocks, with lower numbers of Skylarks and Meadow Pipits.

Earlier in the season is the time for hirundines, with House Martins and Swallows moving through. Their numbers can be very concentrated, or spread over a longer duration. Between mid October and mid November 2017, 12,000 birds were counted by one observer!

The park's local tit flocks are joined by Willow Warblers in August, and later in September/October Chiffchaffs should appear. Autumn is also a good time to see flocks of Mistle Thrushes on the open grass sections gathering together before the winter. Of all the thrush species breeding here Blackbirds are the most numerous. The odd Wheatear turns up, but they prefer the open areas of Blackheath just to the south, as do Whinchats. April and then August/September are the most likely times to see them.

Sparrowhawk is the only breeding raptor. The odd Kestrel or Peregrine makes appearances, and during migration Buzzards will drift over. Tawny Owls are present, but generally remain out of sight during daylight hours. I would never stop looking for them, though: if you find a dozen birds alarming together you may strike gold...

VISITOR INFORMATION
Greenwich Park
Blackheath Gate
Charlton Way
Greenwich
London SE10 8QY

Opens at 6 a.m. and closes at various times.

0300 061 2380
greenwich@royalparks.org.uk

Refreshments: cafés at St Mary's Gate Lodge, Greenwich Royal Observatory and National Maritime Museum

Toilets: in park

Cutty Sark (DLR), Greenwich, Maze Hill and Blackheath (National Rail)

Opposite top: The statue of General Wolfe in Greenwich Park, with the dome of the Observatory behind.

Opposite bottom left: A female Green Woodpecker typically feeding on grass. Listen out for the loud 'yaffling' call, an easy way to locate them.

Opposite bottom right: A Swallow: up at the Observatory is a fine vantage-point from which to observe birds on migration through London.

HORNIMAN MUSEUM & GARDENS

How the world came to Forest Hill – and quite a few birds

The Horniman Museum started with Frederick John Horniman, a Victorian tea trader and philanthropist, travelling widely from Egypt to China to Canada and collecting artefacts, specimens and objects along the way, all with the rather singular mission to 'bring the world to Forest Hill'. As what he amassed progressively overwhelmed the house, his wife is reported to have said, 'Either the collection goes or we do.' So they did, and moved out. A sentiment perhaps my own wife can relate to when it comes to my collection of bird books. . .

We are not here for the museum, which now occupies a grand Arts and Crafts building high on Forest Hill, but it is a great place to visit in itself, with its collection of animal skins, aquarium and, the latest addition, the Butterfly House, which I've yet to visit with the family. The restaurant is very good, too.

It's the museum's gardens that will draw you here, a fabulous viewpoint for looking northwards over London, all the way west to the Thames at Vauxhall, and east to Canary Wharf. The view of this amazing capital city spread out before you is worth the visit in itself! The gardens roll down the hill from the museum almost at the zenith, to the nature trail which runs along the bottom, western edge, and for birdwatching can be a very enjoyable venture.

The mature trees attract a wealth of birds, with Goldfinches breeding in the horse chestnut trees, and Nuthatches to be found too. Great Spotted Woodpecker drum, and twice while leading guided walks I have located active nests of theirs, one next to the toilets, which is not something to be stared at through binoculars. . .

The open grassy areas provide perfect feeding areas for pigeons, and Stock Dove are common. Various thrushes join the party, including breeding Mistle Thrushes and odd Fieldfares or Redwings worm hunting during the winter months. They will often sit up in the trees waiting for the hordes to disappear before returning.

Above: A Fieldfare (on the left) and a Mistle Thrush on the Horniman Museum's grassy slopes. Fieldfares make appearances in the winter and Mistle Thrush breeds here.

Right: A solitary Carrion Crow admires the view from one of the Museum's hanging baskets.

Blackcaps breed along the nature trail, and several birds can be heard trying to out-compete the shouting song of the local Wrens. Other smaller species include Dunnocks in the hedges, Coal Tits in the evergreens and Long-tailed Tits breeding in the deep cover. The scattered conifer trees hold Goldcrest throughout the year, and early in the morning you can hear Song Thrushes singing from the gardens' lower reaches.

Sparrowhawks hunt the area and breed nearby, and the odd Kestrel will make an appearance. On warm days the sky is always worth a scan: during a quick 20-minute break between guided walks here one April I had both Buzzard and Peregrine drifting over! And this, remember, is built-up London, and you can get here on the Overground. . .

VISITOR INFORMATION
100 London Road
Forest Hill
London SE23 3PQ

7.15 a.m. –s unset, Monday – Saturday
8 a.m.–sunset, Sunday

Refreshments: café at museum
Toilets: at museum

Forest Hill (Overground and National Rail), 5–10 minutes

Opposite: The odd Kestrel will put in an appearance - will it hover above its prey?

Above: A Great Spotted Woodpecker nesting in the Museum's grounds.

Right: The Pagoda at the Horniman Museum

SYDENHAM HILL WOOD

A fragment of the ancient woodland that once swathed south London

One of the remaining parts of the Great North Wood, which once stretched from Deptford to Selhurst, this is managed by London Wildlife Trust for wildlife. It was the Trust's first reserve after it was saved from being built on the early 1980s.

It's joined to Dulwich Wood, and is easy to wander around for a short walk. Part of what now looks like – indeed is – a sylvan valley is actually the trackbed of the old railway line to the long-demolished Crystal Palace High-Level Station. During the week the wood can be very busy, but the birds are still here regardless of the noise from the school groups enjoying being out amidst nature.

Forty species of bird are regularly seen here. Typical woodland species include Great Spotted Woodpecker, Nuthatches who make their pipping noise from the tree tops, Treecreeper, Sparrowhawk and Chaffinch. Spring sees the arrival of Chiffchaffs.

The more open areas hold Green Woodpecker too. Full of holly and ivy-covered trees, the site is very good for species feeding on insects, like Goldcrest. In recent winters Firecrest have joined the hunt for tasty morsels.

Hobbys have bred here since 2016, and Kestrels breed in the nearby church steeple but hunt over the Wood. Before the Parakeets arrived an Amazonian Parrot stopped over in 1994!

The summer brings Blackcaps, and the dawn chorus erupts as everyone jumps on the bandwagon to sing in competition for territory and a mate. Song Thrush are joined in the winter by Redwings. The typical species of tit are present, with Blue and Great the commonest and the odd Coal and Long-tailed Tits breeding too.

Wood Pigeons feed on the ground, flying up into the trees when people pass through, only to drop down again almost immediately as they pass by. Stock Doves can be heard throughout the year, but the spring is the peak time for them, as they gently sing from the upper canopy. Tawny Owls are here, and with all this ivy are probably watching the unsuspecting masses below.

Above: Treecreepers are regularly seen in the woods climbing up the trees.

Opposite top right: A Nuthatch, which has the ability to go not just up trees but down them too, unlike woodpeckers or Treecreepers.

Crescent Wood Road
Sydenham Hill
London SE26 6LS
Open all the time

020 7261 0447
020 3897 6151

enquiries@wildlondon.org.uk

Sydenham Hill (National Rail), 10 minutes;
Sydenham (Overground and National Rail), 15
minutes

Opposite left: A Stock Dove peering out of its nest. Listen out for their song, a quiet but intense '*who, who, who, who*!'

Opposite above: Long-Tailed Tits breed in Sydenham Hill Wood.

Right: A Song Thrush singing - smaller and warmer-coloured than a Mistle Thrush. The spots on the chest are shaped like arrow heads and not circular as on a Mistle Thrush.

CRYSTAL PALACE PARK

Shoveler as well as dinosaurs at close hand

With its two cloud-piercing television masts Crystal Palace, atop the ridge of hills curving across south-east London, can be picked out from almost anywhere. The spacious park itself, sloping down the hill from the busy Crystal Palace Parade, was opened in 1854 by Queen Victoria with the relocation of Joseph Paxton's actual 'Crystal Palace' – a vast and spectacular glass pavilion – from Hyde Park after the closure of the 1851 Great Exhibition.

But in 1936 the Crystal Palace was razed to the ground by fire, leaving a few remnant statues and structures. Nowadays the park is best known for its athletics stadium, until the opening of the Olympic Stadium in 2012 the capital's premier athletics arena, and its life-sized model dinosaurs which guard the lower lakes.

As with all green urban spaces, the best are those with as many different habitats as possible, and at Crystal Palace Park it is the water features that most contribute to the impressive variety of wildlife. The lower lakes are larger, and therefore richer in birdlife than the higher fishing lakes, but Cormorants are present on both – they're now so common in London that I almost forget how important it is that such a bird can be attracted into the heart of the capital. Typical species on the lower lakes include Tufted Duck and wintering Shoveler. I wouldn't go so far as to say that an urban environment is actually better for wildlife, but I'd never seen Shoveler coming so close to people to feed before I visited Crystal Palace Park! To watch them, with their spatula-shaped bills, only feet

away is a wonderful experience.

Coot and Moorhens are well represented throughout the year, often fighting for territory in the water, and during the winter months four species of gulls. London doesn't have any rivers gushing out of mountains, so Crystal Palace's Grey Wagtails can be found on any water feature – check around the edges for their constantly pumping tail action.

Pied Wagtails, meanwhile, are invariably attracted to the sweeping open areas of short grass, as are groups of Redwings passing through, which can be found feeding just feet away from the thousands of human users of the park. I had over a hundred on a recent visit, and it was a lovely

VISITOR INFORMATION
Thicket Road
London SE19 2GA

7.30 a.m.–dusk, Monday–Friday
9 a.m.–dusk, weekends and bank holidays

friendsofcpp@gmail.com,
landscape.helpdesk@bromley.gov.uk

Refreshments: café in park
Toilets: in park

Crystal Palace (Overground & National Rail)

Above: No other London park has life-sized models of dinosaurs, the distant relatives of our present-day avian friends.

Right: Redwings pass through the park on migration and can be found lingering in the winter months, sometimes in large numbers.

experience listening to their collective chatter as they talked between feeding forays. Song Thrush breed here, and can be seen on the edges, and Mistle Thrush bound around in the open, flying up to trees to give their rattling call. The park is also great habitat for Green Woodpeckers, normally a very shy species: I've had great views of them in its quiet sections.

The park's mixture of mature deciduous trees and thick evergreen cover means a varied selection of woodlands species can be enjoyed. Great Spotted Woodpeckers and Nuthatches feed in the high reaches of the canopy, while the four common species of Tit (Blue, Great, Coal in the conifers and Long-tailed Tit) can all group together to form a feeding mass.

Once the first half of winter is over, the longer days trigger the breeding season, and birdsong begins to spread – for some species this is this best way to locate them. From March onwards Blackcap numbers swell: they're the dominant warbler here, aside from the odd Chiffchaff. Goldcrest are resident, so the insect-attracting evergreen trees are a goldmine for these hyperactive little birds.

Stock Doves can be found, as in most London parks, with their quiet *who-who-who* song, or gliding in on a display flight with their wings held up high in a prominent V. Newly present in small numbers, again as with so many places across London, are Jackdaws, apparently bidding to colonise our capital again.

Come September the colourful and secretive Jay is generally easier to see, bouncing around looking for food. Listen too for Chaffinches, Greenfinches and the pleasant tinkling song of the Goldfinch – identify the rhythm of the Chaffinch's call, suggests the *Times* sports writer Simon Barnes, by imagining the run-up and delivery stride of a fast bowler. . .

Opposite left: One of the two giant television transmitter masts at Crystal Palace.

Opposite right top: Blackbirds are a common sight in the park.

Above: So are Chaffinches.

SOUTH NORWOOD COUNTRY PARK

An important place for birds since the nineteenth century

The London Borough of Croydon has bird records that date back to the nineteenth century: South Norwood featured in them then, and it remains an important place for birds today. A sewage farm until the 1960s, it's now managed as a country park. (Since it's not out in the country, I assume this odd term denotes a park that hasn't been formally landscaped, so kind of looks like the countryside.) At the south end is a visitor centre.

There are three main features: the lake at the north end, the wetland habitat to the south, and the surrounding scrubland. A substantial tally of birds has been recorded here over the years, but the site is small enough that you can just spend a few hours here, and even a quick poke about will usually generate a good selection of birdlife. As with most of London nowadays you're never far away from the staccato squeaking of Ring-necked Parakeets, which seem to charge out of almost every green space.

The lake is small but has reedbeds fringing it, which increases the diversity of the birdlife. Amazingly, one year the deepest section held wintering Bearded Tits, but they haven't reappeared since, which is such a shame. The usual wildfowl are present, with Coot, Moorhen, Mallard, Tufted Duck and two feral species of geese breeding.

Winter brings in more, including Shoveler, which can peak at 30 birds, and occasionally other species like Teal. The local area shot to fame with wintering Pied-billed Grebe at South Norwood Lake (not the same site but very close), and the country park had a wintering Great Grey Shrike.

Above: A beautiful male Wheatear showing characteristics of the Greenland race. You'll need to be out early, as they can be disturbed by the other users of the park.

The park also has wintering Water Rails: the ditches around the lake are a good place to look, but as you might expect these notoriously skulking birds can be very elusive. Grey Herons winter, and there are normally a few Cormorants hanging about. The summer brings Reed Warblers, plus the odd Reed Bunting.

Directly south of here is a wetland area, with a path that divides it on the east edge, which holds Snipe and more Water Rail. Just as elusive are the Tawny Owls which frequent the more wooded areas along the north edge.

As you'd expect in this wetter habitat, the alder trees attract Siskins in the winter, and a few Lesser Redpolls too. Finches tend to flock up during these colder months, and Greenfinch, Goldfinch and Chaffinch can then stay to breed. The site is great for Song Thrush, and once you hit the new year you can hear these great vocalists pouring out their torrents of song. The few open areas of low grass have Mistle Thrushes breeding, and their prolific cousin the Blackbird frequents most parts, not to mention their aggressive relative, the Robin.

The neighbouring cemetery supports a population of Pheasants, one of a few places in the city for them, and these large, alien-looking invaders can be found screeching their croaky screech if you disturb them.

In the winter months Redwings and Fieldfares are about, for some reason favouring the Pitch & Putt course. Diurnal migrants like Wheatears and Whinchats (who migrate during the day, as opposed to by night, like a Redwing) can drop in.

Then there's both common species of woodpecker, Stock Doves and Wood Pigeons, House Sparrows and Collared Doves and, thanks to the mix of bushes and trees, plenty of warblers – Whitethroat, Lesser Whitethroat, Blackcap and Chiffchaff – and all four common tits. You can still expect Kestrels and Sparrowhawks, too, and hope for Peregrines and Buzzards drifting over – as in so much of the London area they are becoming a common feature up in the sky.

VISITOR INFORMATION
Albert Road
London SE25 4NF

Open from 8 a.m. daily. Closing times vary with season
020 8256 1224
Email: southnorwood@quadron-services.co.uk
southnorwood@quadronservices.co.uk

Toilets: in visitor centre

Harrington Road (Croydon Tramlink)

Opposite: Wood Pigeon can be seen in the trees. The prominent white collar and longer tail separate them from Feral Pigeons.

Above left: Pheasants are found in the adjoining cemetery and spill into the park.

Above right: Buzzards can be seen overhead – look out for their long, broad wings and short-tailed silhouette.

Right: Reed Warblers can be found around the lake edges.

BEDDINGTON FARMLANDS

Clouds of gulls and plenty of rarities at the famous Sewage Farm

This site just south of Mitcham Common has legendary status on the London birding scene, with a colossal list of birds recorded over its long history. Please note that there is currently *no public access* to this site. The sterling volunteers at the Beddington Farm Bird Group do, however, run regular guided walks throughout the year, as well as monitoring the bird population and generating a very impressive annual report. There is a long-standing plan to open the site to the public as a nature reserve.

The facility was previously known as Beddington Sewage Farm, and sewage disposal commenced here back in 1860. By the 1980s the sludge beds used for the process had become an important habitat for migrant waders, and ornithological interest in the site increased. In 1990 a large lake was created, the first permanent body of fresh water for the farm. At the end of this decade gravel extraction began, and subsequently the site was used for landfill too! As if Beddington hasn't already had enough done to it, now an incinerator has been constructed there. In this day and age!

Currently the main features are the two lakes on the west side and the largely capped landfill site. This will eventually become a mixture of healthland and acidic grassland and meadows, while an area of wetland grass and reedbed is currently being created to the north. Beddington used to be a stronghold for Lapwings, but numbers have dwindled; hopefully the wetland grass, together with the addition of predator-proof fencing, will see them bounce back.

The landfill still dominates the bird life present, with clouds of gulls and corvids (Jackdaws and Carrion Crows) wheeling about, and Starlings in numbers sometimes exceeding 1,000 birds. When the gulls are not here, they sit on the Northern Lake, the bigger of the two, like crowds of shoppers waiting for the sales to open. With thousands of gulls present it doesn't surprise me that Beddington regularly gets rare species. Yellow-legged and Caspian Gulls appear,

and no winter passes without a few Iceland Gulls.

This mass occupation of gulls tends to force the wildfowl here to tuck themselves away. These include Gadwall, Teal and Shoveler, and the Teal numbers are most impressive, with counts of over 300 and in previous times exceeding 1,000. In the spring Shelduck numbers peak, and several pairs stay to breed with limited success. Coot numbers build up in the winter, with over 30 pairs nesting here, and with all this wet habitat there are also plenty of Moorhen. Water Rails can be seen in winter on the edge of the reeds.

Over 40 Grey Heron are usually present, and Little Egrets are also present in lower numbers. In fact, back in 1990 I twitched a famous bird that wintered here – this was before we all realised they would become so widespread!

Above left: Beddington's small colony of Tree Sparrows (chestnut crown, white cheeks with a black spot), has declined by large numbers, but just about clings on.

Below left: A few pairs of Reed Buntings still breed.

Opposite: Beddington's landfill site attracts hordes of gulls.

Having the River Wandle running alongside means waders move through Beddington Farmlands every year. Lapwings are the only species still breeding, however, and Redshanks have been lost altogether. Odd attempts to breed are made by Little Ringed Plovers. Common Snipe winter in good numbers – up to 50 – and mixed in with them are Jack Snipe, sometimes reaching double figures, making this a nationally important site for this elusive species.

Recently Little Owls have been sighted increasingly, and several birds are now present. Sparrowhawks and Kestrels are regular raptors, and it's fair to say that these days Buzzards have nearly become an urban species. Both Grey and Pied Wagtail breed, but the Yellow Wagtail has now become just a migrant. Water and Meadow Pipits winter, the latter in good numbers but no longer breeding.

No martins or Swallows breed either, but when they visit to feed or on migration their numbers can still impress. Chats migrate through Beddington, too: Whinchat, Wheatear and Stonechat, with Stonechats staying for the winter, as do Fieldfares and Redwings.

Other important birds to look out for at Beddington in addition to the usual warblers and finches are Cetti's Warblers, which as in so many places around London are building up their numbers (the odd Sedge Warbler still breeds, on the other hand, but the species has nearly disappeared from here), and Linnets: a winter flock can exceed 100, while the breeding population, at just below double figures, is very healthy. Adding to the pattern of contrasting growth and decline at this site, only a single pair of Reed Buntings remains – again a similar story to other local sites.

House Sparrows do well here, but Beddington used to be the epicentre for the capital's Tree Sparrow population. While other colonies disappeared Beddington's continued to grow to be the biggest in south-east England, until their habitat was lost, and the population crashed from 80 pairs in 2010 down to five in 2016.

A year does not go by at Beddington Farmlands without some rare bird turning up, whether it's a brief Glaucous-winged Gull from America, a Citrine Wagtail from the east or a Crane from Europe landing for a few days. We can only hope that it comes to be managed well for wildlife in a way that can be enjoyed by everyone.

VISITOR INFORMATION
Mile Rd
Wallington
CR4 4HS

For membership of the Beddington Farmlands Bird Group go to:
bfnr.org.uk.
Otherwise at the time of publication there are no guided walks for the public – monitor the website for developments.

Hackbridge (National Rail), 5 minutes

MORDEN HALL PARK

Wetland and warblers at the end of the Northern Line

Once a deer park – no deer present these days – Morden Hall Park at the southern terminus of the Northern Line is now a mixture of gardens, rivers, wetlands and woods and managed by the National Trust. The River Wandle meanders along the southern edge and fuels the watermill. It can be a very popular park, so if you want to see birds rather than people you may need to slip away from the masses.

It's the river that provides the greatest interest for the birdwatcher. At the west end of the park it irrigates a patch of wetland which holds various species, including Water Rails throughout the year. They have been seen with young. Kingfishers can be seen anywhere along the river: their sharp call is perhaps the best way to pick them up. In the summer look out for numerous Reed Warblers.

Around the weir and the main buildings you'll find Grey Wagtails, Moorhens, Coots and Mallards. The now-ubiquitous Egyptian Geese are here too.

Following the watercourse to the south-east corner of the park you'll find the heronry, with currently 15 pairs of Grey Herons. Little Egrets winter here and, as with other similar sites across London, they are expected to join the herons and start breeding soon. Quite amazing that this graceful snowy-white bird which, only 25 years ago, was a rare and exotic visitor from southern Europe, is now adorning a park in south-west London.

Where the river dips under the road is a great spot to find the small group of Teal which winter here. They can also be viewed from Morden Road. Check

Above: A graceful Grey Heron – a frequent sight at Morden Hall.

this area for the trilling Little Grebe which breed here.

If you venture over the tram tracks you'll come to a narrow corridor running north up towards Deen City Farm. Here you'll find Whitethroats during the summer months. Other warblers breed across Morden Hall Park: Blackcap, Chiffchaff and Goldcrest. Cetti's Warbler, with their chocolate-brown plumage and unfeasibly loud calls, have just reached here, but could conceivably be all over the place within a few years.

Kestrels and Sparrowhawks breed, and just around the corner at Morden Civic Centre Peregrines do too – they can seen on the Centre's webcam or flying over the park.

Typical woodland species breeding in the park include Green and Great Spotted Woodpeckers, Treecreeper, Nuthatch, four species of Tit, Tawny Owls and the ever-present Stock Doves. During the winter Redwings and Siskin come into the park, and Chiffchaffs too, with their fondness for being close to water. Check the trees for roosting Cormorants and clouds of Jackdaws, which don't feed in the park but regularly travel across it to their communal roosts nearby.

VISITOR INFORMATION
Morden Hall Road
Morden
London SM4 5JD

mordenhallpark@nationaltrust.org.uk
020 8545 6850

Open all the time (cafés from 9 or 10 a.m.)

Refreshments: cafés in park

Toilets: in park

Phipps Bridge (Croydon Tramlink); Morden (Northern Line), 10 minutes

Opposite top: Water Rails are usually seen but not heard – their unearthly squeal is unmistakeable.

Opposite bottom: A female Mallard and her ducklings.

Right: A female Blackcap - the males show the black cap rather than this brown of this female.

BATTERSEA PARK

Teal and duelling Coots in a central London park

Bordering the south bank of the Thames, Battersea Park was opened by Queen Victoria in 1858, and designed by James Pennethorne, who was also responsible for another great nineteenth-century London park, Victoria Park in the East End. Once Battersea Power Station is fully re-developed and open that'll be two attractions to visit in this part of town – and with a convenient new Tube station too. The park's land was previously marshland, and a favoured area for duelling. No duelling these days, unless you include the Coots squabbling over territory on the lake. . .

Battersea Park is the only central London site that regularly holds small numbers of Eurasian Teal – you'll have to go out to East India Dock, the other side of Canary Wharf, for the next nearest – and these pretty little dabbling ducks with their metallic-green head flash and pale yellow bums are always a pleasure to see. Also present on the water are your typical Northern Shoveler and Gadwall, as well as the inevitably thriving Mallards.

The lake has various nooks and crannies areas to conceal wildfowl, and its islands hold one of the few roosting sites for Cormorants in central London. Grey Herons breed on them too, so you are bound to get great views of them. A ringed Heron I once photographed here turned out to have originally been ringed in the park, so it hadn't moved much!

The lake margins hold Grey Wagtails, and their piercing call gives their location away immediately. Despite their bold colours and continuously pumping tails they are easy to walk past.

Above: Grey Wagtails can be seen on the lakes at Battersea Park. They can be mistaken for Yellow Wagtails, but only the rump is yellow; their backs are olive in colour. Yellow Wagtails are now mostly a migrant species in London, while Grey Wagtail is a common and widespread breeding species in our concrete jungle.

It's hard to look at any body of water in the capital without seeing Moorhens or Coots, and Battersea Park is no exception. Both are multi-brooded, so from the spring until the autumn you're likely to find young being fed by adults or older siblings.

The park has a high density of mature trees which, with the odd open patch and a very nice wooded strip on the east side, provides a rich habitat for wildlife. Song Thrushes can be located on bright mornings from the second half of the winter through to the spring – blasts of their repeating song are an easy way to locate them in the dense cover on the eastern edge. You can even pick them up in the autumn feeding on berries on the yew trees. Their larger relative Mistle Thrush can be found in the park's open grass: they're easy to pick up sitting out in the open bolt upright.

Smaller birds are present too: you can find Long-tailed Tit, Coal Tit and Goldcrest amidst the woodland foliage. As with their cousins Blue and Great Tit, mixed flocks appear in early autumn, and only start dispersing as winter ends and everyone starts getting territorial.

Listen up for the drumming of Great Spotted Woodpeckers, who breed here and can be picked up against the continuous squeaking calls of Ring-necked Parakeets. Local Peregrines can be picked up on high buildings overlooking the park, or cruising around on the hunt for their next meal. The prominent tall office building just across the river to the north-east is a favoured roost site for them – I sometimes pick them up here from the train as it pulls out of Victoria.

8 a.m. to dusk.
Refreshments: café in the park
Toilets: in the park
Battersea Park Station (National Rail) 10
minutes

Opposite: Gadwall are found on the lake. Note the black bill and rear, contrasting with the beautiful grey vermiculations on the body.

Right above: A male Shoveler: the spoon-shaped bill makes it very distinctive, and is used to sift through the water in feeding frequently, often while spinning in circles.

Right below: Song Thrush.

ST JAMES'S PARK

Ambassadors from far away in the centre of London

Sandwiched between Buckingham Palace and 10 Downing Street, and overlooked by a striking skyline of onion domes and grand residences, this is the oldest of the Royal Parks, and a lot of history attaches to its wildlife, some of it certainly true, other bits rather harder to verify. It's always busy, and a birdwatcher is likely to be sharing the paths with all manner of civil servants, diplomats and politicians. It's open all the time, though I'm not advocating any midnight visits!

Back in the 1980s you could walk into this park and be swamped by House Sparrows, feeding from your hand and even sitting on your head. Now this species has vanished from the park altogether: as in most of central London their numbers have been decimated.

No-one is quite sure why: theories have been advanced ranging from the pollution from vehicle exhaust fumes to the citywide disappearance of garden hedges. Pockets of them are still scattered around the city, and some districts remain rich in them, but others are now deserts. Today's voracious flocks are the local Starlings: squadrons of them descend on the park patrolling around the edges looking for scraps to eat.

Still present today on the lake are the White Pelicans, which have been in St James's Park since 1664 (not the same individuals: we don't have the oldest birds in the world here!), when the first ever specimen was a gift from the Russian Ambassador. In recent years a couple of mesmerising photographs have gone viral of a coot or pigeon apprehensively peeping out of one of these pelicans' great belly-like beaks, about to make a tasty lunch.

In 1996 a pelican was found exhausted at Southend: once rehabilitated it was taken to London Zoo, where it was identified as a Pink-backed Pelican and given to St James's Park. When I was investigating a record of a White Pelican flying high over Wanstead Park I came across this story, and realised that the St James's Park bird was a White Pelican too, and not a Pink-backed. If you are lucky on a spring visit to the park you can see this big white stealth bomber

Opposite bottom left: Pintail are one of the most beautiful ducks. One of those ringed at St James's Park made it all the way to the Urals in Russia!

Opposite bottom right: London's feral population of Red-crested Pochards, which travel around the capital and the surrounding counties, originated from the captive population, and now breed in several parks in the capital.

VISITOR INFORMATION
5 – midnight

0300 061 2350

Refreshments: St James's Café in park
Toilets: in park

St James's Park (District/Circles Lines); Charing Cross (Northern, Bakerloo Lines, National Rail)

cruising up and down the lake, sometimes at low level but often at a great altitude!

Back to wild stuff – at least, the known wild stuff, as there's a collection of captive wildfowl here too, which means that apart from the Coot and Moorhen any of the ducks or geese may not be wild. But this attracts wild birds too: Mandarins make the odd appearance, as do Gadwall and Shoveler, and every now and then something a bit rarer. Records include Greater Scaup, Garganey and in the 1940s even a Long-tailed Duck! The capital's feral population of Red-crested Pochards – up to 20 birds – can be present, mucking in with the captive ones. Indeed, these birds probably originated from a collection like this and, inadequately pinioned, simply jumped the fence. In the mid-2000s a pair of Eiders in the St James's Park collection bred and produced free-flying young, two of which often disappeared from the park.

During the late twentieth century, the captive birds were ringed by Roy Sanderson, including the young of species like Pintail. Since these were the offspring of captive birds he wasn't sure if he'd get any recoveries – people finding his birds a long way away and sending in the details from the particular ring – but within a few years he received a recovery from the North Kent marshes. This was followed by birds found on the Atlantic coast, and eventually one that had made it as far as the Ural region of Russia! Amazing that captive birds still retained the instinct to migrate long distances like their wild counterparts!

Over the last few winters Kingfishers have been present on the east island, and Water Rails can occasionally be seen in the reedbeds but the latter isn't easy. In the summer Reed Warblers appear, but the population is small.

You'll also find Grey Herons and Cormorants, neither of which currently breed here, while Little and Great Crested Grebe are present during the winter and sometimes into the summer as well.

Being so close to the River Thames we are always joined by gulls here: Herring, Lesser Black-backed, Common and Black-headed in the winter; during the summer we lose the last two, smaller ones.

Opposite top: A mighty White Pelican. Nowhere else in London can you see such an avian phenomenon!

HYDE PARK & KENSINGTON GARDENS

Taylor Swift not the only Swift to have appeared here

These two parks really form one huge green space separated by the West Carriage Drive – oddly, the large lake that bisects them has two different names depending on which park you're in!

Kensington Gardens was once the back garden of Kensington Palace, but not these days, though it remains the official London residence of junior royals like the Duke and Duchess of Cambridge (Prince William and Princess Kate to you and me).

Hyde Park is the largest central London Royal Park and, despite hosting vast open-air concerts by everyone from Taylor Swift to the Stones, the Winter Wonderland funfair, an art gallery and open-water swimming and welcoming over 7 million visitors a year, still manages to accommodate loads of wildlife. It's a real melting pot of activities, but that's not why I go there!

For birdwatching I would suggest keeping to the water, which means the conjoined Serpentine and Long Water (which the Serpentine becomes once you cross the bridge!) plus the solitary Round Pond. The birds are all over but, with boats for hire on the Serpentine, perhaps more abundant on the Long Water, though I think you get closer views on the Serpentine.

The Serpentine is a real magnet for birds, with the newly created reedbeds now holding Reed Warblers and the odd Sedge Warbler, plus the latest colonist, Cetti's Warbler, which you can hear throughout the year. There are only a few here, though, so they're not constantly singing in competition with one another.

With water comes wildfowl, so expect the common spread at your feet of Tufted Duck and Pochard with lower numbers of Gadwall and Mandarin Ducks. As autumn lands Shoveler appear, along with the feral and ever-increasing Red-crested Pochards. Little and Great Crested Grebes breed, the latter often appearing along the shoreline. Cormorants don't breed, but are another very close bird whether roosting or feeding.

Grey Herons have started breeding here now, and walk around the water's edge as though they're part of the furniture. Every now and then other birds turn up, with Teal and Wigeon most winters, and sometimes something tasty like a long-staying Scaup and even Goldeneye!

Other water visitors include the common species of gull, which are joined by the odd Yellow-legged Gull, and once a Ring-billed Gull on the Round Pond. This is not really a site for terns, so it was amazing that one White-winged Black Tern stayed just over a week. The shoreline is great for Grey Wagtails throughout the year, and Pied Wagtails frequent the short grass areas too – you'll even find them feeding by the Round Pond, which is surprisingly good for birds, given how barren it looks. Kingfishers are about, but don't breed yet. . .

Swifts appear above during the summer, and House Martins breed nearby so will always be about. In the spring and autumn Swallows, plus the odd Sand Martins, appear, sometimes en masse above the lakes, a wonderful sight.

Sparrowhawks breed here, and with several pairs of Kestrels in the area, they can be seen overhead and also roosting on the buildings to the south. Both Tawny and Little Owls breed – Tawny used to be visible in the trees west of the Peter Pan statue, but now rarely show. Little Owls are easier to see, and

Kensington Gardens is a good area to search, but due to disturbance from photographers I'm not going to reveal any specific locations.

Kensington Garden is better for woodlands species: Great Spotted Woodpecker, Nuthatch and, just about, Treecreeper. The Nuthatches come to the feeders west of the Long Water, and you'll probably see people feeding the Ring-necked Parakeets around here too. Blue, Great and Coal Tit all breed and come to the feeders. Long-tailed Tits are also breeding and appear almost anywhere. In the early spring Song Thrushes will be singing, but outside this time I've found them nearly impossible to find here, unlike Mistle Thrushes, which parade around the short grass.

Among the warblers only Blackcap and Goldcrest breed, with Chiffchaff and Willow Warbler only migrating through. Spotted Flycatcher used to be a breeding species here, but no more.

VISITOR INFORMATION
5 a.m. to midnight

Refreshments: several cafés in park
Toilets: in park

Marble Arch, Lancaster Gate, Hyde Park Corner and Knightsbridge Tube stations

Above left: A Mute Swan in mid-landing on the Round Pond.

Opposite below: A Great Crested Grebe chick in Hyde Park.

Left: Swifts boomerang about the skies high above Hyde Park during the summer months.

THE REGENT'S PARK

Waterfowl and woodland birds in a surprisingly tranquil setting

People have been watching birds in the Regent's Park (as it's officially called) for years, and for a public park it has a phenomenally long list of species – exceeding 200. Some of the park staff, who are on site nearly all the time, have contributed to this: in 2016 Dave Johnson and Tony Duckett saw a Cory's Shearwater flying over – a remarkable record!

Originally called Marylebone Park, it was used first for hunting, then farming, and wasn't opened to the public until 1835. It stretches all the way from the Marylebone Road up to Camden Town and Primrose Hill, and has somehow maintained a tranquillity none of the others quite matches, despite containing everything from football and cricket pitches to beautiful formal gardens and an open-air theatre. There are several cafés, and the one called The Hub, high on a mound at the north end of the Park looking out towards London Zoo's Mappin Terraces, is a suntrap in summer.

But for birds you can focus your attention on a few areas. This lovely park can be enjoyed throughout the year, and no matter how long you have there will always be something to see.

The large lake along the park's western edge is possibly its main feature, with what might be the world's tamest Grey Herons, which are frequently out on the shore and nearby grass throughout the year. They return to breed from January, and you'll see pairs displaying and building their nest on both islands, although the north island has the main population. The southern island has a very low nest on its west side which is a great photograph opportunity.

As well as the usual Canada and Greylag Geese, there is a growing population of Egyptian Geese – an introduced species originally in wildfowl collections but now established in feral populations. In the park, numbers are on the up.

Other water birds also breed: Great Crested Grebes, Little Grebes, Moorhen, Coots, Mallards, Tufted Ducks and Pochards. Gadwall and Shoveler swell the numbers from July. Odd birds turn

up and even stay for long periods, like the Greater Scaup which graced the park for 16 years! In the northern inlet of the lake beyond the Long Bridge is a collection of more exotic wildfowl like Smew and Wood Duck – another place where you'll need to check the wings to see what is free-flying! Red-Crested Pochard are here breeding as feral birds, however, and can be seen throughout the year as they move between the Royal Parks.

An unusual winter species for central London is Water Rail: with several pockets of reedbeds around the lake several birds are often present, and now they have their own feeding station, on the edge of the reedbed just north of the boat house. These lovely reedbeds also support a small population of Reed Warbler, frequently joined in the spring by the odd territorial Sedge Warbler. Reed Bunting do appear and can linger, but have yet to be confirmed as a breeding species.

Cormorants frequent the lake, and up to 70 birds will roost here overnight! Gulls breed, with Herring and Lesser Black-backed on one of the islands that do consume the odd young water bird. . . In the winter Black-headed and Common Gull join the masses, and the odd Yellow-legged Gull turns up.

The well-vegetated, more formal area inside the Inner Circle is a great spot for breeding Song Thrush, and provides a wealth of food for both Goldcrests and the odd Firecrest. Just to show how birds can turn up anywhere, in 2003 the small ornamental lake was frequented by a Lesser Scaup!

Blackbirds hop about in most areas, while Mistle Thrush normally stick to the short flat grassland. During the winter more thrushes appear, including Redwings, and spring and autumn migrants may include Whinchats and Wheatears, the latter also favouring the open grass. The breeding population of Stock Dove and Green Woodpeckers can still be connected with in across the park out the open.

The area north of the lake lake has bird feeders, and the tree-hugging Great Spotted Woodpecker, another breeding species, will come down to them. The four common species of Tit feed here as do Greenfinch, Goldfinch and Chaffinch. Blackcaps breed as do

Above: Tawny Owls breed in Regent's Park.

Opposite above: Great Crested Grebe can usually be found on the lake.

Opposite below: The non-native, tree-nesting Egyptian Goose are present in Regent's Park. Their numbers continue to grow across the capital.

Chiffchaff, and occasionally the odd Whitethroat. Look out, too, for Green Woodpeckers and Stock Doves.

Just west of here are several large nest boxes which Kestrels breed in, and the park supports two pairs of Sparrowhawks. The old golf and tennis school in the north-west corner, now called a Chat Enclosure, is also worth exploring. Both Little and Tawny Owl breed in Regent's Park, but are hard to see. With the Little Owls there is some chance of success, but with the Tawny Owl being almost completely nocturnal you will be very fortunate.

VISITOR INFORMATION
Regent's Park Office
The Store Yard
Inner Circle
Regent's Park
London
NW1 4NR

Open from 5 a.m.; see website for closing times

0300 061 2300
regents@royalparks.org.uk

Refreshments: several cafés in park
Toilets: throughout park

Great Portland Street or Baker Street (Metropolitan, Hammersmith & City and Circle Lines), Camden Town (Northern Line), 5–10 minutes

HOLLAND PARK

Tawny Owls tucked away in a sylvan oasis

When I first started birdwatching in the 1980s, I remember, I watched an elderly gentleman in Holland Park feeding Jays by hand. An amazing sight, and I've never seen such a thing again.

Then again, this this beautiful, sylvan London park always feels a little bit out on its own. It may be just a few steps off busy Kensington High Street, and nowadays have the new Design Museum in the former Commonwealth Institute building at its portal, as well as opera in the open air every summer, but every time I visit it still feels deliciously hidden away. The real jewel of the site keeps a particularly low profile. Holland House was built in the seventeenth century as Cope Castle, then bombed in the Second World War, and its ruin is obscured amidst the wood.

There is an ecology centre which runs various events with assistance from the Friends of Holland Park, and has information on what wildlife's about and bird feeders outside. Add in playgrounds, toilets, an Orangery with regular art exhibitions, a café and even a restaurant, and it's hard to imagine there isn't something for everyone here.

The park is in two sections: an open area to the south for recreational activities, and to the north a tranquil wooded section that runs all the way through to the neighbourhood of Holland Park. This northern section is a rich habitat that is carefully looked after, with lots of areas fenced off to prevent them being trampled or disturbed by dogs, for example.

In the winter this provides masses of food and cover for birds, but it's the breeding season that makes clear just how important such an environment is.

When I surveyed Holland Park back in 2009 its avian population was more than 300 total pairs, which is a huge amount of bird life for its acreage.

The most dominant species are Wrens and Robins, making up nearly a third of that population, and any early-morning wander around here will bring you evidence of them. Tawny Owls breed, and in the first light of day can still be heard with their trying to out-compete the cacophony of dawn chorus. The rare moments when all the birds suddenly go silent, on the other hand, may indicate one of the breeding Sparrowhawks is out hunting the rides.

Opposite above: The formal walled garden in Holland Park. There are bird feeders on the right hand side of the picture which Nuthatches and Coal Tits regularly come down to feed on.

Opposite below: Sparrowhawks breed in Holland Park and can be spotted charging through the foliage hunting unsuspecting birds. . .

Blackcaps and Song Thrushes are two a penny throughout the park, but you need to be early to catch the Song Thrush singing. Four species of Tit are present, with good numbers of Coal Tits – Blue Tit size, but no blue or yellow on them – as they have lots of conifers to keep them happy. Together with the large number of holly trees these provide the small Goldcrest population with enough food.

Two species of woodpecker are present, and one year, while leading a guided walk here, I discovered a pair of Green Woodpeckers excavating a new nest site beside one of the playgrounds, as close by the local human population went obliviously about its business. Nuthatches are present, but only the odd pair, so require some searching out. Stock Doves are common, and frequent the bare branches of the upper canopy or can be found amongst the common Wood Pigeons feeding on the floor of the woods.

Various small ponds attract Mallards and Moorhens to breed, and it's not too uncommon to find a long-legged Grey Heron in search of prey here too. Nowadays the noisy Egyptian Geese are joining in the fun, as these tree-nesting geese can be high up as well as low down.

Blackbirds toss the leaf litter about looking for a tasty morsel, and are joined in the winter by Redwings and normally Chaffinches as well. In the autumn Jays are normally more obvious, gathering a winter crop trying to make sure the pesky Grey Squirrels don't get them all.

Migrants do make appearances in Holland Park, including warblers you'd expect such as Lesser Whitethroat. But one year a Reed Warbler was found here which, given there isn't any typical habitat for this species, illustrates just how precious this island of green just off the A4 is for food-starved migrants.

VISITOR INFORMATION
Ilchester Place
W8 6LU

7.30 a.m. until half an hour before dusk
Refreshments: café in park
Toilets: in park

High Street Kensington (District and Circle Line)
12 minutes

Opposite: Tawny Owls breed in the park but you'll need to be crepuscular by nature to hear them. Joining a dawn chorus walk here is usually early enough to hear one in the spring.

Right above: Robins are common in Holland Park.

Right below: Coal Tits - the smallest of the four common tits - are present in good numbers.

LONDON WETLAND CENTRE

The WWT's fabulous memorial to Sir Peter Scott in west London

Each of the main wildlife conservation charities in London has a large nature reserve devoted to birds: the RSPB's is at Rainham Marshes, another is the new Walthamstow Wetlands, managed by the London Wildlife Trust in conjunction with the London Borough of Waltham Forest and still a work in progress, and the third is the London Wetland Centre at Barnes, the only Wildfowl and Wetlands Trust reserve in the London area – and what a place it is.

If you are more than three decades old you may remember this site when it was still four square working reservoirs for Thames Water, called Barn Elms Reservoirs, named after the stately home that was here until it was destroyed by fire.

The Wildfowl and Wetlands Trust was founded by the great naturalist Sir Peter Scott, and established its first reserve at Slimbridge in Gloucestershire, and it was his dream that one day there should be a similar refuge for birds in the capital. Well, the Wetland Centre is the posthumous result, opening in 2000 and flourishing ever since. So total has been the transformation of the site that only in a few places can you still see the remains of the grassy slopes of the old reservoirs.

In their place is a network of wetland habitats, an impressive visitor centre including educational facilities, a shop, a specialist binoculars and telescope retailer and a very nice café. Just be aware that the price of admission is not cheap. The approach here is more markedly educational, with a conspicuous amount of information provided about the wildlife present, the

history of the reserve and the WWT's work.

Even the small lakes near the entrance gather wildfowl, so it's possible to start birdwatching from the moment you arrive, and the buildings themselves hold breeding birds – both Blue Tits and Pied Wagtails, for example, regularly nest in the courtyard.

The reserve is split into two sections, and the west and the south routes round each have their own hides, with views across the various areas of wetland from the main lake to reedbeds to wader scrapes and even a grazing marsh.

The west route takes you through the pens holding a collection of captive wildfowl – a practice unique to the WWT among wildlife charities – to a patch of trees that are good for Goldcrest. Sparrow-hawks have bred here, and in the winter look out for Goldfinch, Siskin and Lesser Redpoll feeding. The Headley Discovery Hide gives great views across the main lake, where Common Terns breed. In winter the reedbeds here yield Bitterns – up to six across the reserve, a remarkable achievement for inner London – and have even been heard booming in the spring before they depart. At this reserve you're never far from reeds, and they may pop up anywhere around it.

Beyond this hide lies the Wildside Hide which towers up into the sky. I love a multi-levelled hide, and here we have two, hh-mmm. From the upper level you get great views across the grazing marsh, which is full of wildfowl during the winter, and in the spring and autumn a great place to see Yellow Wagtails and Wheatears as they stop over. In the winter it's a regular spot for Stonechats, too.

An impressive catalogue of warblers breed here, including Whitethroat, Lesser Whitethroat and Sedge Warbler, and the ideal habitat has attracted the ever-increasing Cetti's Warbler – I recall hearing some

VISITOR INFORMATION
Queen Elizabeth's Walk
Barnes, London
SW13 9WT

020 8409 4400
info.london@wwt.org.uk

Refreshments: café in visitor centre
Toilets: in visitor centre

Barnes or Barnes Bridge (National Rail), 15 minutes; 485 bus direct to reserve (not Sundays or bank holidays)

Opposite: The Lesser Redpoll is an acrobatic little finch with a roseate cap and black bib.

Right above: Wheatears make an appearance on migration at the Wetland Centre, like this female.

Right below: The Sedge Warbler has a prominent stripe over the eye and an explosive, fast song.

singing one year beside the car park: another lovely experience in the heart of the capital.

The south route has four hides, two of which, Dulverton and WWF, overlook the main lake. Large gulls sometimes congregate here, including on a regular basis Yellow-legged and Caspian Gulls. Most of the wintering wildfowl will be represented, with good numbers of Wigeon, Gadwall, Shoveler, Teal, Pochard and Tufted Duck. Shoveler use the site as a staging post during the autumn and spring, reaching several hundred birds. During the breeding season Gadwall, Shoveler and even Teal have hatched out a brood here! Great Crested and Little Grebes are present all year and breed, though the more secretive Little Grebe is harder to find. In winter Lapwing numbers build up, and both Snipe and Jack Snipe are present, though seeing them is another matter.

On the eastern side of the reserve the Peacock Tower looms up, with three levels, of which only the upper two are accessible. From here you can scan the top of the Charing Cross Hospital at

Above right: Among the exceedingly rare visitors to the Wetland Centre was a Night Heron.

Hammersmith for Peregrines, who do make appearances over the reserve, and it's also good for viewing the breeding waders, with Lapwing, Redshank and the odd Little Ringed Plovers fighting to defend their young against the marauding gulls. When I was volunteering here back in late April 2012, someone called out as an Iceland Gull glided past.

South-east of here is the artificial nest bank for Sand Martins; numbers vary from year to year, but recently it has been full to the rafters, making this arguably the most reliable place in London to see this species.

Already an impressive list of really rare birds has turned up at the Wetland Centre – Pacific Golden Plover, Bluethroat, Little Bittern, Night Heron –and Avocets have attempted to breed. Within living memory, Avocets were a bird you had to travel to Suffolk and take a boat out to Havergate Island to see – now they come up the Thames. Whenever you visit you should see something, and it might be something special.

Above: Who'd have thought you'd be able to see Avocets within London? At the Wetlands Centre they have bred, but the young never made it.

RICHMOND PARK

Deer and even Dartford Warbler amidst London's largest green space

Richmond Park is the largest green space in London, and the second largest urban park in the whole of Europe. It's easy to lose yourself in it and forget you're still in the capital (at least until an airliner thunders over on its approach to Heathrow). With an amazing and famous view from King Henry's Mound across London all the way to St Paul's Cathedral – developers are still not allowed today to build anything that would obstruct this view – it's always worth a trip, whether you are interested in the wildlife or not, and several places to eat and a good spread of amenities make it a one-stop shop for a day out. Being so large means it abuts several different neighbourhoods, and is therefore well served by public transport.

For most visitors, the park's sizeable herds of Red and Fallow Deer will be the initial attraction, and you will get some magnificently close views. Their presence goes all the way back to 1625, when the transformation of this green space into a deer park with no public access did not go down well with the locals. All that has since changed, and nowadays the park has been designated as a Site of Special Scientific Interest and a National Nature Reserve.

Despite their tame appearance the deer in Richmond Park are wild animals. *Do not approach too closely*, as they are still dangerous, especially in the rutting season, and people are still injured from time to time through not keeping their distance. The only time the park is closed is in February and November when the deer are culled (see the park's website for more details).

Now to the birds! Possibly the two most abundant species in the park are the Ring-necked Parakeets, which flood into the trees, and Jackdaws, almost carpeting the ground in packs to feed. Both species make lots of noise, but the jack call of the Jackdaws is perhaps one of my favourite bird calls. These delightful Jackdaws take advantage of Richmond Park's massive array of trees to breed

Above: The Dartford Warbler is a very distinctive bird, and best located by its quiet, churring call, or by its associating with Stonechats.

Left: The glamorous male Mandarin can been seen at Pen Ponds in the middle of the park.

Richmond Park
Holly Lodge
Richmond Park
Surrey
TW10 5HS

Open from 7 a.m. (7.30 in winter)

0300 061 2200
richmond@royalparks.org.uk

Refreshments: cafés and restaurant in park
Toilets: in park

Richmond (National Rail, Overground and
District Line)

in, and can be found on the backs of the deer picking off insects – a sight more like something out of the Serengeti than south-west London.

Pen Ponds, at the heart of the park, provide a great attraction to wildfowl, and especially the feral population of Mandarin Ducks. These ducks, originally from China, adapted so well to the UK once they'd escaped from bird collections that at one point numbers were higher than the dwindling native population! Mandarins are tree-nesters, so don't be too surprised to find these ducks up a tree or walking through the woods with their young!

Most common species of duck are present in low numbers, including Wigeon, Gadwall and Shoveler. Water Rails can be heard calling, Kingfishers can be found, and Great Crested Grebe are here all year round and breed. During the summer Sand Martins breed too, as do a few Reed Warblers.

As you'd expect from the clusters of tree and scrubland, once winter ends they become alive with singing birds. Song Thrushes start off, and then come the migrants: Blackcaps, Whitethroat, swelling numbers of Chiffchaff, and lower numbers of Garden Warbler. Goldcrest breed predominantly in the conifers scattered across the park.

One of Richmond Park's most important selling-points when it comes to birds is the numbers of breeding Stonechat. This is one of the few places within London still attracting this attractive little bird, generally associated more with open country and heathland. Up to a dozen birds breed here, producing excellent clutches of young most years.

During the winter months the Stonechats are often joined by Dartford Warblers, even more of a heathland-dwelling bird and perhaps even more re-markable within Greater London – not so long ago the

main population was confined to the Dorset and the Surrey heathlands. Check the large areas of bracken for them, including those by Pen Ponds. Perhaps the creation of some characteristic habitat for them – patches of gorse, for example – might encourage them to stay on to breed one year. . .

Migrants do turn up in the park, with regular Whinchat and Wheatears which, as you'd expect with the sheer numbers of visitors and dog-walkers, are subject to disturbance. Ring Ouzels and Redstarts are less frequent. In October 2017 some 880 Chaffinch flew through in the late morning.

Richmond Park's woods are full of birds that attract raptors – the four species of tit plus Nuthatches and Treecreepers – and besides the Kestrels and Sparrowhawks, and Hobbys hunting over the lakes in summer, Buzzards are now breeding here.

There are also two species of owl breeding, with both Tawny and Little Owls exceeding 20 pairs.

As well as the two common species of woodpecker, the increasingly rare Lesser Spotted were still hanging on until recent years. A few pairs of Swallow breed, helped by the abundant supply of damselflies and dragonflies.

Above: The Serengeti? No! Richmond Park. Jackdaws (identifiable by their grey heads and silver eyes) sit on the deer picking insects off them.

Right: Little Owls are not completely nocturnal, unlike Tawny Owls, so you can pick them up in the trees during the day. Listen out for their cat-like *meow* call at dusk.

WORMWOOD SCRUBS

A great place for chats; Soviet spy preferred Moscow

Famous for the prison – but we'll give that a swerve! HMP Wormwood Scrubs, which overlooks the southern edge of this 200-acre open space, is one of London's Victorian-era prisons, with its distinctive castellated architecture, and hit the news in 1966 when the Soviet spy George Blake was audaciously sprung from it and spirited away to Moscow.

VISITOR INFORMATION
Open all year round

East Acton (Central Line)

After the First World War, the open space was originally an airship station, then allotments during the last war, and thereafter used by the Ministry of Defence (MoD) as a training ground. In 2002 'The Scrubs', as it is locally known, was designated as a Local Nature Reserve, and is strongly protected. It's also the local patch of the original Urban Birder, David Lindo. Here is where he first learned to look at birds in the middle of the city. Given the hordes of dog walkers that use the space too, earlier is better for birdwatching.

Wormwood Scrubs consists of grassland intersected with scrub, with narrow wooded sections around the perimeter. This is a great habitat for Song Thrushes, best heard early in the morning, with a few singing later on. Dunnocks and Wren are common, and in the summer compete with Whitethroats, which bound into the sky on their display flights. The thicker areas hold Blackcaps and Chiff-chaffs, with the odd skulking Lesser Whitethroat thrown in for good measure. Willow Warblers migrate through, but no longer breed.

The areas of scrub are real heaven for Linnets, and the muscular Greenfinches describe circular patterns in the sky with their bat-like display flights, singing their nasal trills and wheezes. Goldfinch is the latest species to explode on the scene.

Wormwood Scrubs is a great place for chats. Whinchats are the commonest on migration, followed by Wheatears, and later on Stonechats, with the odd bird wintering, too. Ring Ouzels – think Blackbird with a white bib, the thrush of the uplands – even make appearances, as do Redstarts: there was one famous bird in 2004–5 that wintered here!

Opposite left: Redstarts are possible at Wormwood Scrubs, like this male. One famous bird even wintered here!

Opposite right: A male Stonechat. This species is normally associated with heathland: check any stretches of tall grass for them.

Above left: Linnets can be found at the Scrubs. Note the male's pink-hued breast, which becomes brighter during the spring/summer.

Above right: HMP Wormwood Scrubs, beyond the nature reserve.

Left: Whinchats are another chat that turns up at Wormwood Scrubs.

Opposite below: Tree Pipits often visit in autumn.

Meadow Pipits were once a regular breeding species here, but are now only just holding on, with the odd bird present in spring and summer and a few wintering. Tree Pipits are regular in the autumn but, as in the rest of London, by no means reliable.

The odd Reed Buntings make appearances and sometimes summer here. With all the vegetation come invertebrates and their predators: Green Woodpeckers and, in the wooded areas, Great Spotted Woodpeckers.

In the sky above Swifts return late in the season for a short duration before heading south again for the winter. Kestrels love it here, and can normally be found hovering. Sparrowhawks are present, too, and it's worth checking the chimney of Hammersmith Hospital to the south as Peregrines sit up there. The hospital also provides nesting spaces for Starlings, which drop onto the Scrubs searching for food. The neighbouring streets still harbour House Sparrows, which sometimes venture into the south-west corner of the park.

During the autumn Redwings and Fieldfare move through, with some wintering birds favouring the Linford Christie Stadium area to the south. Winter also brings gulls, which wander around trying to avoid the other recreational activities. The local Carrion Crow flocks, with their mob-like antics, exceed a hundred birds. At dusk Ring-necked Parakeets crash here for the night, and have peaked at no fewer than 5,000! They used to favour the central wood but have now dispersed around the edges.

Rare birds have turned up from time to time at the Scrubs, including Common Rosefinch, a few Richard's Pipits and even an Ortolan Bunting. Perhaps the future will see Cetti's Warbler establish itself: in 2017 one sang here for four weeks. . .

BEDFONT LAKES COUNTRY PARK

A rare place in west London to see Bitterns and Smew

Another place whose usage has changed several times over the years, Bedfont, in the shadow of Heathrow, was originally farmland, then used for gravel extraction, then turned over to landfill, until Hounslow Council created what you see today: a pleasant country park. It may not be the biggest site for birdwatching in the capital, but it does contain several different types of habitat, so in a short walk there's the chance of seeing a good variety of birds. The park is on the edge of a very populated area, however, and can get busy, here so the earlier you're here the better. And it does offers the prospect of at least two absolute stars.

The first is Smew, the small sawbilled duck from the Baltic and further north, whose male, with its snow-white plumage and black-streaked head is sensationally beautiful, and once seen never forgotten. Britain sees small numbers turn up each winter, no more than a handful at most in any one location, and a few have been coming to Bedfont. They generally arrive late and leave early, so it's a narrow window to see them: December to January is the best time. To the west of London the next nearest place for Smew would be Wraysbury, out near Windsor, and to the east you'll have to go up to the Lea Valley, or all the way to Dungeness. . .

For many years Bedfont has also held Bitterns, the dumpy brown herons that even until recent years used to be incredibly rare all over Britain. Up to two birds have been seen here at once, so all the reed-fringed lakes are worth a good look. You may well hear this secretive species rather than see it, and once you've heard its extraordinary, mournful 'booming', like a tugboat horn on a foggy ocean, you'll always remember it.

These reeds also hold Water Rails, which usually skulk away invisibly, but are possibly easiest to see on frozen mornings when they are forced out into the open to feed.

Most common wildfowl are present in low numbers, and

mixed with them the odd Great Crested Grebe and Cormorants. When I visited a short while ago a pair of Grey Herons were nesting on one of the islands, so hopefully this is the shape of things to come.

As the days become longer summer migrants stream into the country, Bedfont's more open areas fill up with warblers: Reed Warbler, Garden Warbler, Whitethroat, Lesser Whitethroat and Blackcap. Chiffchaffs breed. So do Skylarks, but as this species is in decline the small area of this reserve means it is hard to know for how long. Whinchats are also regular migrants, and Stonechats turn up from time to time.

Keep your eyes skyward as Kestrels and Sparrowhawks are knocking about, and Buzzards and Red Kites frequently drift over.

Following the Warblers come the Common Terns, to breed on the tern rafts. Fighting for space on them are Black-headed Gulls. Kingfishers are present the whole year, streaks of electric blue dashing across the lakes. In the summer Hobbys feed over the lakes too.

The Common Tern chicks are ringed, and provide invaluable information on the destinations and distances our birds travel on migration. Imagine flying south for the winter all the way to southern Africa, and then returning to the UK every year to breed!

Opposite top: A male Smew. They winter here in very small numbers, a stunning bird to see. Bedfont is one of the few places in the capital they still visit.

Opposite bottom left: Skylarks breed in small numbers on the reserve, though, as elsewhere, numbers are in decline.

Opposite bottom right: Lesser Whitethroat is one of the many warblers breeding at Bedfont. Listen out for the song, a rattle all on one note. They can be very elusive.

VISITOR INFORMATION
Clockhouse Lane
Bedfont
Feltham
TW14 8QA

0845 456 2796

8 a.m. to 5.30/6 p.m.

Toilets: on reserve

Ashford Station (National Rail) ,15 minutes

STAINES RESERVOIR

Not the most scenic stroll, but amazing winter visitors

This is hardly the place for a nice Sunday afternoon walk, or somewhere to take the kids on a bank holiday. In fact, bounded by the thunderous M25 and screamed over by jets coming in to Heathrow, it is a pretty bleak place.

But birds don't know that, and for the serious birder it can be extremely rewarding – especially, being so exposed (another reason to choose somewhere else for a sylvan stroll), when the wind picks up! Staines boasts a long list of rare birds, most of them waders when the water levels are right: they include Collared Pratincole, two Wilson's Pharalopes, a wintering Baird's Sandpiper, seven Kentish Plovers and Sooty Tern, to name a few. As recently as 2017/18 a Horned Lark wintered, well showing characteristics of this north American version of the European Shore Lark!

Despite the name there are actually two reservoirs, the North and South Basins, built in 1901, separated by a causeway along which the public footpath is the principal viewpoint for the birder. Originally there was public access all the way round, but that didn't last.

Grass, water and concrete is pretty much all there is here, at least until one of the reservoir's water level is lowered for maintenance work and brackish pools appear. Sometimes the site then dries out too quickly, which isn't that attractive for birds, but sometimes it is just right and they flock in. When the vegetation grows up it provides feeding habitat for finches, and when the reservoir is filled up with water again ducks descend in their hundreds.

These luxurious moments are few and far between, at least ten years apart. Since both basins have been drained recently, it is unlikely to happen again soon.

So back to the concrete bowls of water: they still pull in the birds and, like all reservoir-watching, it can be hard at times, or really magical. On the north basin there are two tern rafts, mostly

now used by Black-headed Gulls, though a few Common Terns do still breed there. Odd things do turn up on them – I once saw a Sanderling sitting on one in October.

The edges of the reservoirs attract waders, which sometimes frequent the causeway, affording excellent views. These vary from Dunlin to Oystercatchers to Whimbrel to Little Ringed Plovers. Tern migration can be seen here too, with Arctic, Common and Black Terns, plus the odd mingling Little Gulls.

Staines is a great place to see duck. Large numbers of Tufted Duck are present from July, and in September Shoveler numbers build up to several hundred. Garganey, a dainty and quite rare little duck with its white-striped head, are found in the autumn too. In the winter Wigeon move in to feed on grassy banks, and by the spring Goldeneye, with their unique blunt heads, are already displaying at one another, getting ready to depart to breed further north.

It's unusual for something rare not to appear in the winter, whether a Slavonian Grebe or a Great Northern Diver, which can be surprisingly hard to locate when actively feeding. How do you tell one from a Cormorant? Look out for their pale dagger shaped bill, white face and front half of the neck. Great Crested Grebes are always present at Staines, and smaller Black-necked Grebe are seen nearly every month, peaking at about half a dozen.

Gull numbers increase from July, when Yellow-legged Gulls can turn up, often on the jetty on the adjacent King George VI Reservoir to the west. Mediterranean Gulls are winter visitors – one used to winter on the east side of the north basin, disappearing to the recreation ground to the east.

It's now common see Red Kites, with their characteristic forked tails, drifting over, moving ever

Opposite: These birders are looking at something else whilst these Yellow Wagtails perch on the railings.

Above: A stunning Great Northern Diver which stayed long enough to moult into summer plumage. Not present every year, but they do make regular appearances.

Right: Meadow Pipits breed in long vegetation across the country, but during the winter and on migration can be found on the banks of reservoirs in small flocks.

VISITOR INFORMATION
Grid ref: TQ 0529 7323

Causeway open at all times

Refreshments: café in Tesco Extra, Ashford

Ashford or Staines Stations (National Rail),
20 minutes

further into west London from where they were
reintroduced in the Chilterns, as well as the odd
Kestrel or Peregrine. In late spring there can be can
be thousands of Swifts zipping around swooping
up insects on the wing, and such large numbers of
hirundines can attract Hobbys.

With the insects come wagtails and pipits. Rock
Pipits head north in March, followed by White and
Yellow Wagtails, with frequent Wheatears. If the grass
on the banks is long enough Meadow Pipits can be
present throughout the winter. In the autumn they all
head back south, and can be seen very well along the
causeway.

Opposite top: This vision of loveliness in beige, a juvenile
Ruff, feeds along the concrete edge of the reservoir. Even
without any mud to feed on, waders are still attracted to
the site.

Opposite bottom: Flocks of Wigeon winter at Staines feeding on the grassy banks. The yellow blaze on the foreheads of
the males is characteristic, as is their call, a piercing whistle.

CASSIOBURY PARK

Red kites overhead at this remnant of classical parkland in Metroland

Right at the north-west corner of Greater London is Watford. Still served by a branch of the Metropolitan Line, it is very accessible, and so what better than visiting the historic Cassiobury Park?

For over 250 years it was the home of the Earl of Essex (Why didn't the Earl of Essex live in Essex? I don't get it), but in 1916 the 7th Earl was run over by a taxi and died of his injuries. Death duties made his widow sell off the grand mansion with its magnificent Baroque interiors. In 1927 it was demolished and most of the parkland redeveloped for housing, leaving 190 acres as a public park.

Our main focus is the west end of the park, where the Grand Union Canal runs north-south and Whippendell Woods borders it to the north. This area is designated a nature reserve and managed by the Herts and Middlesex Wildlife Trust. There is a hide with a feeding station in front of it, always a bonus.

There's also a small network of waterways, mostly wooded, with some open areas too. Walking down from the east side, just before you reach the water, you'll see a patch of trees scattered across the grass, an essential place to look for Little Owls throughout the year. In fact, you are right next to the Gade Avenue car park, which is a good spot for Lesser Spotted Woodpeckers. This secretive species of woodpecker still holds on here, so listen for its longer, quieter drumming. It would be great if this population survives.

This is not a place for masses of wildfowl, but you do get a lot of M's – Mallard, Moorhen plus a small population of Mandarin Ducks. When I re-visited the site for the first time in nearly 30 years, on the fishing lake at the south end we saw two Coots, which are rare here, but maybe the shape of things to come.

But what blew me away immediately on this visit to Cassiobury was the near-constant presence of Red Kites. That it would not be considered unusual to see several birds in the air at once as they

VISITOR INFORMATION
Cassiobury Park Ave
Watford WD18 7LB

Open all the time

01923 226400

Refreshments: cafés in park
Toilets: in park

Watford (Metropolitan Line),
2 minutes

Opposite top: Red Kites have steadily spread west from the Chilterns, where they were originally re-introduced. At Cassiobury they frequent the skies on a daily basis. Note the distinctive long, forked tail, and large white patches on the underwing.

drifted over the site illustrates what an excellent conservation success Red Kites are. Re-introduction not far away from Cassiobury in the Chilterns, from where they have steadily spread outwards and around the M25, has not only brought them back from the edge of extinction in this country, but in less than three decades has also seen the population flourish, with 50 pairs now up to over 1,800! Red Kites continue to spread: you'll see them over Reading town centre, over the Weald in East Sussex, and venturing further and further into London itself.

The woods here are bordered by more woodland: hence the wonderful population of Great Spotted Woodpeckers, Nuthatches and Treecreepers. The summer pulls in Blackcaps and Chiffchaffs plus the odd Whitethroat, and Lesser Whitethroat and Willow Warbler on migration join the masses too. At night Tawny Owls can be heard, as you'd expect from such mature trees present. If you wander up to Whippendell Woods you'll get more of the same tree-dwelling species.

Above: House Martins breed at Cassiobury in the summer: their all-white body when seen from underneath differentiates them from the dark-throated Swallow and the all-dark, sickle-shaped Swift.

Cassiobury was once the site of watercress beds and, though they have long since become overgrown, the Water Rails which lurked in the cress beds are still present, now hidden in the masses of cover along the water edges.

This has become a good area for Bullfinches, too, as it is full of scrub and old hedgerows. In the winter Siskins come down to reside here – in fact this was the very first place I ever saw them! Alders provide great feeding places for them. The networks of water frequently attract Grey Wagtails.

Song Thrush can be found in the more scrubby sections, whilst Mistle Thrush favour the open grass of the main park – in the autumn as post-breed flocks gather together their numbers can exceed 30. Winter is also great for Redwings, with the peak count being 1,200 – just a few!

Jackdaws have spread here, as they have elsewhere, and hundreds can be encountered at a time. The wood and scrubland is also great for Jays and, as you'd expect with this species, they are significantly easier to see in the autumn than during the breeding season.

Both House Martins and Swallows breed in the summer, and this brings in the odd Hobby. On the raptor front Buzzards and Sparrowhawks breed here or nearby, and in Watford town Peregrines are present. Find me a town that won't soon have Peregrines!

Above: A male Great Spotted Woodpecker, with the red nape patch, feeding young at the nest.

Opposite: A Waxwing gorging on berries and displaying its punk-like crest.

Some birds are just a wonderful to see. The eye-catching highwayman's mask, the punky quiff, the intricate wing pattern, including the small bright red waxy feathers, the high-pitched trilling call. . . Or just the way they stuff their faces with berries like they are going out of fashion.

Waxwings are prone to influxes in the winter. No two years are the same, but the tell-tale signs are hundreds if not thousands flooding into Scotland in November, indicating either a good breeding season, or that the winter berry crop in Scandinavia has failed and they need to travel further in search of food.

Here in the capital the excitement doesn't normally kick off until the second half of winter,

so from January onwards I start the hunt for my Mohican-sporting friends. My first Waxwing I discovered in 1989 from the top deck of a number 34 on my way to college in Barnet. I left my then-girlfriend and jumped off to watch this little Starling-shaped bird stuff berry after berry down its throat.

So the best tip I can give you is to look at every flock of birds in the tops of bushes or trees that resemble Starlings. Especially if they all suddenly descend for a berryfest. They don't seem to prefer any specific trees or bushes: when you're hungry you eat what you can. Luckily, many car parks are planted with berry-bearing bushes.

GROVELANDS PARK

Mandarin Duck in a Humphry Repton landscape

This park in north London between Southgate and Winchmore Hill is full of history. Originally it was part of the royal hunting forest; then, in the late eighteenth century, it became the grounds of Southgate Lodge, a mansion designed by John Nash for a wealthy local brewer, with the great landscape designer Humphry Repton laying out the gardens. In 1911 the park was purchased by the local council, and the Great War saw the house used as military hospital – nowadays it is a private clinic.

But what may appear these days to be just another municipal park actually holds a wealth of birds. The main attraction, and reason for coming here to look at birds, are the strikingly beautiful Mandarin Duck, originally from East Asia, a feral population of which became established in Britain in the last century, almost certainly after escaping from a collection. At Grovelands their numbers balloon during the winter months, and the last fading of the light is a great time to watch as they gather together with the odd bout of displaying as the males strut their stuff to the females.

The London population of Mandarin is poorly monitored, so it's hard to know quite how many are present, and the numbers gathering in the winter are considerably higher than those that are recorded breeding. This most likely reflects their preference to breed in trees away from water. At Grovelands the winter population has exceed 180 birds!

The lake also has the normal suspects present: Common Coot, Eurasian Moorhen and Mallard, while Shoveler, Tufted Duck and Common Pochard also appear here during the winter. Great Crested Grebes are also present and sometimes breed, as do Little Grebes. You'll also see Cormorants and Grey Herons, and I recall during the late 1980s coming here to photograph a handsome male Red-breasted Merganser, which you'd normally expect to see on a lake up in the mountains rather than one in a north London park. To my displeasure the Ring-necked Parakeets have penetrated here too,

Above: Grey Wagtails are often found by the stream running through the park.

Opposite right: Mandarin Duck are a dazzling addition to the lake in the park.

Opposite left: A Chiffchaff will sing its name, '*chiff, chaff, chiff, chaff*'. They can be found throughout the year, whereas the similar-looking Willow Warbler is a summer visitor only present from April to September.

and can be found in the trees.

A stream feeds out of the lake at the northern end and cuts through the wooded section of the park. As with all streams in London, Grey Wagtails are often present. The wood is full of mature trees, including a large section of holly. Holly is great for providing cover for birds and, as an evergreen with leaves all year round, conserves warmth, which retains insects for longer periods, in turn pulling in Goldcrests. For numerous winters Grovelands Park has also been a regular spot for Firecrest. Great Spotted Woodpeckers and Nuthatches are here, too, but knowing their call is essential to pick out these tree-dwelling species.

As you'd expect from woodland with plenty of low cover, Stock Doves live high up in it, and Song Thrush occupy the lower levels. Blackcaps can be found in summer, and Chiffchaffs singing their own name add to the wealth of birds present.

VISITOR INFORMATION
44 Queen Elizabeth's Drive
N14 6RD

Open 8 a.m. (Mon – Sat), 8.30 a.m. (Sun)

020 8379 1000

Refreshments: café in park
Toilets: in park

Southgate Station (Piccadily Line) or Winchmore Hill (National Rail)

Above: Nuthatches are easier to locate once you know their various far-reaching honking-like calls that echo through the woods. Listen for the soft trilling song they utter in the spring.

QUEEN'S WOOD & HIGHGATE WOOD

The dawn chorus in ancient woods

These two adjoining woods are one of my favourite places in London to lead a dawn-chorus walk. If you've never done such a thing I fully recommend the crazy-o'clock start time required: you'll soon join the converted. These are rich and beautiful woods, among the five in north London classed as ancient woodland, dating back over 500 years and teeming with life, and on a still, cloudless morning you can be swamped by a deafening eruption of song. The peak month is April, but from January onwards the number of singing birds rapidly increases to peak in May/June as they rush to rear their offspring.

Arriving before first light gives the best chance of seeing the Tawny Owls resident in both woods, especially from January to March before the trees sprout their leaves. Dusk is always good for hearing them: a good spot is along Wood Lane and Wood Vale in Queen's Wood, where you can even listen from the comfort of a car. During one overcast April walk I looked up and a Short-eared Owl drifted over.

Redwings are present during the winter, gathering in flocks towards its end. Flocks of Great, Blue and Long-tailed Tits move through, the woods often alive with them as they practise singing before heading to northern Europe to breed. January/February is best for Great Spotted Woodpeckers drumming. From April Blackcaps turn up, preferring the more open sections of the woods.

Sparrowhawks breed, but with all the leaf cover can be difficult to see. In recent years Kestrels have bred in a nestbox at the north end of Highgate Wood.

Above: A stunning male Goldcrest displaying his bright orange/red crown; females have yellow crowns. Check all evergreen trees and bushes for this delightful bird.

VISITOR INFORMATION
Queen's Wood
Muswell Hill Road
London N10
City of London Corporation

Highgate Wood
2 Sheppards Cottages
Muswell Hill Road
London N10 3JN

highgate.wood@cityoflondon.gov.uk
020 8444 6129
07786 538 932

Queen's Wood always open; Highgate Wood from
7.30 a.m.

Refreshments: Highgate Wood Café in middle of
Highgate Wood

Highgate Station (Northern Line)

Left: A Treecreeper with its intricate brown-and-white
plumage on the upperside, which makes it hard to see.
White on the underside makes it easier. Listen for their
high pitched 'srri' call.

Opposite: This Black Redstart was photographed in 1951
by the pioneering bird photographer Eric Hosking nesting
in a bombed-out building near St Paul's Cathedral.

Landmark London Birds: **BLACK REDSTART**

The Second World War left the capital with many bombsites, like the Barbican. Suddenly Black Redstarts began to breed on them: these barren, flattened areas of scattered vegetation mimicked the mountain slopes of their breeding habitats in mainland Europe.

In the near-continent they're widespread across cities, towns and villages, but here they go for the urban setting. The massive spread of redevelopment across the capital, however, has seen numbers decrease. It's not the nest sites they can't find – they'll nest deep within air-conditioning units on the tops of tall buildings or in fire-escape stairwells – but the feeding habitat: they need to eat too.

I first encountered them at the factories west of the King George V Reservoirs in north London. On bright sunny spring mornings males would sing from the tallest buildings, odd birds feeding on the banks of the reservoirs. That population has disappeared.

Now perhaps your best chance in the capital is to hear one singing early in the morning. But males may not sing on consecutive days, so finding them is not easy. In 2017 a male sang most mornings from the Houses of Parliament –perhaps not the best place to be wandering around with a pair of binoculars! Listen for their jangling song, mixed with rasping notes, that has a very eerie quality to it.

HAMPSTEAD HEATH

One of London's biggest and most magnificent 'green lungs' is also excellent for birds

Hampstead Heath dates back a few years: it was first mentioned in the history books back in 986! Originally privately owned, it was eventually purchased by the Corporation of London in 1888. Kenwood House, the mansion at its northern tip, was acquired for the nation in 1928, and the result, preserved for ever as public open space, was what we know as Hampstead Heath today.

This magnificent tract of grassland, woodland, lakes and ponds and sandy heath stretches for nearly 800 acres, is some of the highest ground in London and, in Parliament Hill at the southern end, has one of the finest vantage-points from which to behold the capital. It also has a lido, the legendary bathing ponds for men and women (people were 'wild-swimming' here long before the term was even invented), a running track, open-air concerts in summer and a wonderful art collection. It's one of London's most glorious and precious green lungs.

Very little of the original heath is left, but work has been going on to restore some of the original wildlife habitat. In 2015 work to restore the ponds at the Highgate edge dredged up an entire Ford Cortina (the UK's biggest-selling car in the 1970s). No-one knows how it ended up there: it could have been in its watery grave for over 50 years!

Enough about rustic lumps of metal: we're here for the birds, and a remarkable array of rare species have turned up over the years, as its most famous local birder, Bill Oddie, will attest, from a Little Bittern on summer evening on a small landscaped pond in the company of Moorhens, to an adult male Lesser Kestrel drifting around one late morning in spring while the rest of the country was enjoying an influx of Red-footed Falcons, and a lovely Alpine Swift which stayed for a week in 2006. What next?

The main areas to concentrate on are Parliament Hill for watching migrants, the Highgate and Hampstead Ponds for

VISITOR INFORMATION
Open all the time
hampstead.heath@cityoflondon.
gov.uk
020 7332 3322

Refreshments: cafés at Kenwood
House and Parliament Hill Fields
Toilets: at Kenwood and Parliament
Hill Fields

Hampstead Heath (Overground),
5 minutes; Hampstead (Northern
Line), 10 minutes

Previous page: London blinks out into the dawn, seen from Parliament Hill. Get to the Heath around this time before the dog-walkers do to see more birds.

Opposite above: A frosty morning on the Heath.

Opposite below left: A Willow Warbler on spring migration. August is the best time to look for them.

Opposite below right: Look out for Blackcaps on the Heath, like this female.

wildfowl, and finally Kenwood for woodland birds. Let's start on top of the world with Parliament Hill: this is where migration can be witnessed at first-hand.

Spring isn't that is easy to predict, so let's focus on the autumn. That starts with Tree Pipits in late August, then Meadow Pipits push through in September, followed by Skylarks in October, and finally the thrushes and Wood Pigeons. Clear skies are not helpful for seeing them, as birds tend to gain altitude, so try for days with some cloud about. Sometimes in September the sky can filled with Swallows as they wait before moving on.

The finch migration can be great too: in October 2017 I logged over 500 Chaffinches plus over 40 Hawfinches moving through in a single morning. It can be noisy here at this popular viewpoint, so the earlier the better, and while the crowds are taking in the prospect of the BT Tower and Canary Wharf you may need to stand a few metres away to be able to hear anything avian.

You will see several rows of enormous trees nearby: these have sprouted from very mature hedgerows. Their quieter edges are worth walking along for migrants such as warblers and flycatchers – in August the site can be very good for Willow Warblers. Also from August check through any stretches of long grass dotted with vegetation for Whinchats and Wheatears – towards the Cricket Pitch from Parliament Hill is a great spot for them.

The interlinking ponds on the east side of the Heath, the Highgate Ponds, are good for wildfowl, but some species like Pochards, a rare bird for here, stay shy of them. Check out the southernmost lake, which is good for Shoveler and, most years, Gadwall too. Great Crested Grebe breed on these, and Tufted Duck are common. The more hidden Sanctuary Pond is great for Siskins in the tall alders and a prime site for Water Rail: to see them is harder than hearing their unearthly squeal.

Kingfishers breed on the Heath, so check over hanging branches for them on any of the ponds. Cormorants can be found on most stretches of water. Stock Pond is great for Mandarin Ducks, which have moved in over recent decades, as is the northernmost pond, and the ponds at Kenwood. Check out any reeds, as Reed

Warbler breed on several of the ponds.

As the days become longer from the end of the winter summer migrants return. Blackcaps are common, with a few pairs of Chiffchaff and Whitethroats breeding too. Whitethroats can be found up on top of Parliament Hill. Throughout the year you can encounter Goldcrest, which also breeds here.

Raptors are abundant: several pairs of Kestrel still breeding, Sparrowhawks present in the wooded areas and local Peregrines making appearances. Buzzards are common migrants overhead, and Red Kites move through in April and May. Some years Hobbys show well, but are not predictable.

At the northern end of the Heath is Kenwood which, as with any wood in London, is full of birds. Tawny Owls breed, although wandering around here at night may not be an enjoyable experience. Great Spotted Woodpeckers, Nuthatches and Treecreepers are all present, along with the four common species of tit, Jays and Jackdaws, the latter quite recent arrivals. Where the open fields meet hedgerows is good for spotting Song Thrush, while Mistle Thrushes prefer to be out in the open.

To the west of Kenwood as you head downhill towards Hampstead village and Hampstead Heath Overground Station you'll come across the Hampstead Ponds. You won't see wildfowl in the numbers present at some other sites, but they're always worth a look for a perched Kingfisher or a feeding Great Crested Grebe. Common Terns don't breed here but do skim down to the water to feed. Now head back up onto Parliament Hill for one last fabulous view out across the capital.

Opposite top right: Hobbys can be seen hunting hirundines (swallows and martins) on the Heath. They will also hunt in gardens like a Sparrowhawk, flushing up birds for their dinner.

Opposite bottom right: Ducks on one of the Highgate Ponds.

Above: Towards the cricket field near Parliament Hill is a good place to search the long grass for Whinchats.

BIG WOOD

Escape like the bird life into an ancient wood in north London

Sandwiched amidst a very posh part of north London, and officially designated a Local Nature Reserve, this ancient wood is twinned with Little Wood, which lies just to the north-west.

Nearly square in shape, the wood is dense with mature trees stretching up to the sky. The beauty of it is that it has a circular solid path all the way round it, very easy on the feet. There is an outer trail too, which is muddy and for the more adventurous explorers. If it wasn't for the drone of airliners on flight paths to distant countries, you could almost feel you had escaped from London.

As you'd expect from any richly natural urban environment, the wildlife streams here as towards a safe haven. This is an under-watched site, so detailed information about its changing bird population is thin on the ground, but the bottom line is that there are lots of good birds to see here.

There's a high density of breeding birds, kicking off early in the year with drumming woodpeckers from January, and accelerating from February as the dawn chorus gathers. Song Thrushes, Blackbirds, Robin, Wrens, Great Tit, Blue Tit and Woodpigeon have the highest numbers, all exceeding double figures, whilst Great Spotted Woodpeckers, Stock Dove, Song Thrush help to keep the wood at maximum capacity.

The verdant surroundings pull in breeding Nuthatches, and the odd Treecreeper still hangs on. In the summer Blackcaps storm in and take up residence, the only summer visitors. The periphery is worth exploring, too, as Dunnocks prefer the transitional habitat between wood to garden; the odd Greenfinch and Goldfinch can be found here too. Spring and summer see bird numbers at their height, especially early in the summer months.

Tawny Owls and Sparrowhawks breed here or nearby. Both Wood Pigeon and Stock Dove reside in good numbers, the Stock Doves' '*who-who-who*' song perhaps the best way to locate them in the upper canopy. One spring day a Cuckoo spent the morning here in Big Wood, so you never know what you might bump into. . .

VISITOR INFORMATION

Temple Fortune Hill
Hampstead Garden Suburb
NW11 7XR

Open all the time.

Golders Green (Northern Line), 15 minutes

Opposite: Wrens are one of the many typical woodland species abundant in this ancient wood.

Above: The odd Greenfinch can be found on the fringes of the wood, like this male.

Left: Dunnocks also prefer the edges of the wood and can heard singing from neighbouring gardens.

Opposite: A House Sparrow, increasingly rare in the capital these days.

In the late 1970s House Sparrows were, as the saying goes, two a penny – so many I recall being frightened by them as they landed on people in the Royal Parks to feed from the hand. They were so common we took them for granted.

By the 1990s numbers had started to drop. People complained they had hardly any House Sparrows in their gardens. By the 2000s they had almost completely vanished from central London.

What happened?

There are many theories, but from my observations one thing became clear: we were getting rid of important habitat for them. They like roofs with holes in them, gardens with big thick bushes to roost in, and hedgerows full of insects to feed their young on. London is losing all of these all the time. They have lost breeding sites, roosting sites and feeding sites. Being a very social bird, once one pair goes others, soon follow.

So what can we do? Help them in your garden: nest boxes for sparrows by your roof, an evergreen bush for them to roost in, and how about a bird table with some nice mixed seed for dinner? With this, we may still be able to keep the House Sparrow in London.

COLDFALL WOOD

An ancient woodland in north London alive with birdsong

Yet another still-standing ancient wood in North London, bordering Muswell Hill and East Finchley. Would you believe it dates back fully 450,000 years, to when glaciers reached southern England: it was right here, from just a few pieces of rock found and analysed, that this amazing piece of information was deduced!

The first round of coppicing (the planned thinning-out of trees to allow vegetation to grow underneath and around them) has now been completed here, which has increased the biodiversity of the site, so species not normally associated with woods are present, including Dunnocks in these open sections.

Coldfall is also edged by housing, a cemetery and allotments, which no doubt add different habitats to attract wildlife. As a result House Sparrows are still present, and can be found in the gardens at the northern end.

Birding in woods like this can be hard work in winter, as they tend to have more disturbance from human visitors with their dogs, and earlier in the day will increase your chances of bumping into wintering mixed flocks of Great, Coal, Blue and Long-tailed Tits as they charge around searching for food. The ever-present Great and Blue Tits are probably the commonest breeding species.

Flocks of Chaffinches can be present, spread across the green and brown carpets of mixed leaf-and-brush debris.

Great Spotted Woodpeckers do well here, and birds can be heard drumming in the very early part of the spring. Song Thrushes enjoy the mix of vegetation

here too, and singing males shout their repeating song in the early mornings as the sun kisses the horizon. Mistle Thrushes find the open spaces ideal feeding areas meanwhile, and they too can be found singing in the spring. Blackcaps and Chiffchaff jump in from April onwards, and are spread throughout the wood. Even the odd Willow Warbler stops off on the way north to sing as well.

Nuthatches will be singing in the spring, and Treecreepers used to be present, but I haven't seen them in recent years – they were down to just the odd bird. Wrens and Robins appear to sing from most of the wood.

This is a great place for catching a glimpse of a Jay and, if the heavens look down fondly on you, you may encounter them singing too, or even displaying in small groups, their crowns raised up like elongated Mohicans. In fact, if you really want to appreciate the wonder of birdsong and identify all the sounds around you, then join one of the bird walks here.

VISITOR INFORMATION
Creighton Avenue
N10 1NS

Open all the time

East Finchley (Northern Line), 20 minutes

Above: Jays really are the most beautiful of the corvids (crows). Despite their loud screeching calls, their song is a soft array of complex whistles and clicks.

Opposite above: Great Tits are widespread throughout the wood, uttering their repeating 'peter, peter, peter' song.
Opposite below: Here a male Blue Tit sings for a partner. Another common species in the wood.

WILLIAM GIRLING RESERVOIR

A vast reservoir that attracts vast numbers of gulls and rare waders

Situated between Chingford and Enfield, this is the largest single reservoir in the Lea Valley. It is twinned with the King George V Reservoir, and together they supply a great deal of the capital's water. The man who has been immortalised in history by having a vast stretch of water named after him was a chairman of the Metropolitan Water Board.

Currently there is *no public access* to the reservoir, but it is viewable from Mansfield Park, Chingford just to the east. Recently, however, there has been a movement within Thames Water towards arranging more access to sites managed by them, so in future we all may be able to see this magnificent reservoir up close.

Work began on its construction in 1936 but, owing to various technical issues and the interruption of the Second World War, was not completed until 1951. During the 1940s, while it was being built, Little Ringed Plovers bred here: it was only in 1938 that they started breeding anywhere in the UK. Given their preference for large flat open areas covered in rubble, it's no surprise that this massive construction site took their fancy.

The reservoir is long and oddly triangular in shape, and it is possibly its sheer length that is the main attraction for birds. The winter months see it frequented by wildfowl, and at dusk the main attraction arrives: gulls – thousands of them, as many as 20,000 at a time.

During the 1990s when I had access to this site it was commonplace to find Mediterranean Gulls and Yellow-legged Gulls in the increasingly gloomy light as the sun disappeared behind the horizon. On my second visit for the gull roost – my first was a failure, as I arrived too late to see anything – I found an adult Iceland Gull, which at the time was the first adult ever seen in the Lea Valley. So you can see why I like this reservoir.

During the early 2000s William Girling hit the headlines with nationally important levels of Black-necked Grebes present. They

Above left: Tufted Ducks can peak at 1,000 birds during the early autumn, having arrived in the capital in July to moult.

Above right: Two Purple Sandpipers were seen here in 1991, a very rare wader inland. One was found by the author.

Left: The reservoirs hold nationally important numbers of Black-necked Grebes, which can exceed over 30 birds.

Opposite: Slavonian Grebes are among the five grebes that can make an appearance on the site.

had frequently turned up here for many decades, and a small flock would winter here. By the end of the 1990s the number was into double figures. Nothing massive, but since then it has has steadily climbed, and in the autumn of 2013 peaked at 42. These can be picked up from Mansfield Park with a telescope, and there have been various open days at the reservoir when better views have been had.

Numbers of wildfowl present are normally low, with the exception of Tufted Duck, whose numbers can peak at over 1,000 birds. Goldeneye are present from November onwards, and Goosander are still encountered here, but their numbers are lower compared to peaks in the 1980s and 1990s. In the spring breeding Shelduck return to breed, then disperse elsewhere rapidly.

Around the site run flood-relief channels, and when the water levels in these are low they can attract the odd wader. In 1991 during a cold snap these held Dunlin, several Snipe, a few Jack Snipe and some crowd-pulling Purple Sandpiper. The reservoir attracts wading birds regardless of the water levels present, and one autumn over two days three different Pectoral Sandpipers were found.

One of the interesting features about this reservoir is that it has an internal maintenance road running inside the reservoir. Most of the time this is underwater, but when water levels drop it becomes exposed. As waves crash over it they can leave a muddy shoreline which is a magnet to any shorebird.

This reservoir has a long list of rare birds that have graced its water, from a flock of seven Velvet Scoter to White-winged Black Tern, to Avocets to Long-tailed Skuas to three species of Diver, and all five common species of Grebe. You never know what will be next. . .

VISITOR INFORMATION
(view from)
King's Head Hill or
Mansfield Park
Chingford
E4 7SP

No public access (view from Mansfield Park or the road). More details from the Thames Water website

Chingford (Overground), 10 minutes; Ponders End (National Rail), 5 minutes

RIVER LEE COUNTRY PARK

Everything from Nightingales to Otters around this mosaic of lakes

Cutting north out of London is the Lea Valley, which holds a vast array of possible places to see birds – we could fill most of this book with them. At just 30 minutes by train from Liverpool Street to Cheshunt, however, the River Lee Country Park, with its mosaic of flooded gravel pits, is a very tempting outing. (Another approach is by road via Waltham Abbey to park at the big Fishers Green car park on the eastern edge of the site.)

The gravel extraction stopped many years ago, way before I ever ventured this way, and now the pits are substantial lakes frequented by everything from sailing dinghies (at the top end) to otters. There are a great many lakes here, all situated among pleasant woodland punctuated by stretches of grassland, and although they are well signposted the paths are quite a maze, so I would equip yourself with the map on the River Lee Country Park website or available at Fishers Green. Allow at least half a day to walk round, as the lakes are spread out over quite a substantial area.

Two species of bird in particular are great to see, and at different times of the year: Bitterns winter here – they were already coming to the Lee Valley even when the species was still exceedingly rare across most of the country – and in the spring Nightingales sing to their hearts' content.

Bitterns are present from November through to February at least, and the best place to see them – the clue is in the title – is the Bittern Watch Point on Seventy Acre Pit. This is north-east from Cheshunt Station, and the hide is on the far side of the lake. First and last light are great times to see these stubby brown herons, but they will appear throughout the day: you just may need to wait. But don't worry: Water Rails are normally pattering in and out of the reeds as something else to watch.

Another great attraction of this Country Park is the large number of wildfowl, with good numbers of diving ducks like Tufted Duck and Pochard, plus the dabbling ducks: Teal, Gadwall,

Above: Bitterns are one of the star attractions at the River Lee Country Park.

Right: They even have their own hide to watch them from.

Shoveler and Wigeon. Lower numbers of Goosander and Goldeneye (in winter) can be seen on almost any of the lakes, but Holyfield Lake, the northernmost and largest, is the most likely. The summer also brings breeding Black-headed Gulls and Common Terns.

Smew are also present during the winter, again usually only on Holyfield Lake, but in increasingly low numbers – recent winters have only produced a single bird. Gone, it seems, are the glory days when Smew in double figures were not unexpected! Then again, even a single Smew around London is worth an outing.

Just south of Holyfield Lake is an area of trees and scrub, and this is where to find the Nightingales – around the electricity substation is a good spot to look. The Nightingale is another species far from common these days in Britain, and unfortunately declining, so any chance to see this extraordinary and legendary bird is one to take.

Early in the season is best, from late April until early May, when they can be heard singing their extraordinary, voluptuous song – once heard, never forgotten, and worth travelling a long way for! – and even seen (usually deep within a bush, but look out for the rufous rump). They are still around into June, but by then singing more at dawn and dusk.

The lovely mixture of trees also provides food for finches, with good numbers of Siskin and lower number of Lesser Redpolls present during the winter, and from late spring the whole area is normally alive with the chorus of numerous species of warbler, including Garden Warblers, Whitethroats and Chiffchaffs, while the newly created reedbeds hold Reed and Sedge Warblers.

Throughout the year you should be able to pick up the ubiquitous Cetti's Warbler, with its explosive song, but somewhat more retiring behaviour.

Even if you don't look for a single bird, on a nice day the River Lee Country Park is a lovely place to walk round, but if you do, you should find a great deal more.

Left above: Otters are present in the Lea Valley but rarely seen. It's possible to see the evidence of their presence in their fishy-smelling spraint (poo) on the banks of the pits or other waterways that cut across the area.

Left below: Nightingales have become more localised in the South-east these days. Singing mainly in April and May, they can be real skulkers, but are easier to spot earlier in season when there is less foliage.

Above: Common Terns breed here in the summer. Watch them skimming down the surface of the water.

Right: Goldeneye are present in small numbers in the winter, and before they leave you can sometimes catch the males displaying to the females by throwing their heads back and forth.

KING GEORGE V RESERVOIRS

Vast numbers of wildfowl where country meets city

The King George V Reservoirs got their name simply by being opened by King George V. Completed in 1912, they were split into two because of concern that on such a long single body of water the waves would get too high.

Access is possible with an annual permit which is issued at Walthamstow Wetlands immediately to the south, along with a key to get you in. At these reservoirs we really do separate the city from the country: due east is the northern tip of Epping Forest; there is farmland to the north, but to the south you can still see Docklands.

These reservoirs, along with the William Girling Reservoir next door – collectively they are known as the Chingford Reservoirs – are nationally important for the large numbers of wildfowl. Tufted Duck and Goosander numbers have exceeded the nationally important number, but the latter's numbers have recently dwindled.

Massive numbers of roosting gulls stream in to gather on the King George before departing for the William Girling. Yellow-legged and Mediterranean Gulls racing against the failing light are regular, and when they were watched on a regular basis the odd Iceland and Glaucous Gull also turned up. The gull roost can exceed 70,000 birds, and floats on the water like a sprawling iceberg.

In the winter wildfowl numbers increase, with Goldeneye joining the Goosander. The lack of any vegetated margins means Great Crested Grebes don't breed here, but do spend the summer. Black-necked Grebe are found primarily on the William Girling, but the odd bird does appear on the King George.

From July Tufted Duck numbers increase, followed by Shoveler in August and Teal from October. Oddities also turn up, with Garganey and Scaup (think bigger version of a Tufted, but silver back and no tuft) recorded most years.

Common Scoter, a proper seagoing duck usually far out on the oceans, migrate through in low numbers, only staying a day or two, but have reached 65 and stayed weeks. During the winter the rarer grebes turn up, and sometimes the odd diver, normally a Great Northern. Large number of Cormorants sometimes roost on the side of the reservoirs.

Opposite bottom left: Common Scoter frequently turn up on spring migration in varying numbers, and have stayed for over a week.

Opposite bottom right: A Goldeneye taking off.

KING GEORGE V RESERVOIRS 181

As spring kicks in Wheatears appear on the banks and groups of pipits (nearly all Meadows) and wagtails feed on the grassy banks. These bring in Yellow Wagtails in good numbers, and lower numbers of Pied Wagtails. The Rock Pipits which appear on the edge of the water in March are Scandinavian birds heading back north to breed.

From April Terns start to move through, with Common Terns the most prevalent, but north-west winds can see Arctic Terns take over in numbers over a hundred in a day. Black Terns are normally later. All this water sees waders appearing too, especially Little Ringed Plovers and Common Sandpiper.

Near the end of the spring Swift numbers can build up, and in early June reach several thousand, in large feeding frenzies as low clouds push all the aerially-borne insects lower – often passing within inches of you.

Autumn for birdwatchers always starts early, and by July Common Sandpipers can reach double figures. Other waders appear – Dunlin, Sanderling and Turnstone – particularly with overcast weather or low water levels.

More autumn migrants include Yellow Wagtails and Wheatears moving to the warmer parts of the globe. Oddly Whinchat are more frequent here in the autumn, and can be found feeding off the fences. But migration can be a real hit-and-miss affair: sometimes clouds of birds descend to gain extra energy, and I've seen these King George V Reservoirs teeming with Swallows and Martins feeding low over the water or migrating south, and hundreds of terns.

King George V has an impressive list of rare birds, from long-staying Long-tailed Skuas to Spotted Sandpipers and Citrine Wagtails: you never know what you'll find. . .

VISITOR INFORMATION
Lea Valley Road
Chingford
London E4 7PX

Access by permit only, obtainable from Thames Water.

Ponders End (National Rail), 15 minutes

Opposite: A male Smew flying. Birds often turn up here during cold snaps.

Above: A Sabine's Gull is among the reservoir's rare visitors.

Right: Goosander – from the same family of sawbilled-ducks as Smew – join the Goldeneye in winter. Only a few decades ago large numbers would gather on the reservoir at dusk; now it is good if they reach double figures.

WALTHAMSTOW WETLANDS

The largest urban wetland in Europe

This vast new reserve in north-east London was opened in 2017 by the London Borough of Waltham Forest and Thames Water in association with London Wildlife Trust. Covering 211 hectares, across the ten working reservoirs that are still supplying water to over 3 million Londoners, it's the largest urban wetland in Europe, no less. Now with a plethora of facilities, including possibly the nicest toilets I've encountered at any reserve (in their old incarnation they were truly shocking!), it's a must for any birdwatcher.

A Site of Special Scientific Interest (SSSI) for its large heronries (among the top five in the country for breeding Grey Herons), and at over 2,000 birds a nationally important area for moulting Tufted Ducks, it also falls under the Special Protection Area (SPA) for the Lea Valley for its significant share of north-west Europe's winter population of Northern Shoveler and Gadwall. This is a really important site for wildlife, not just in Britain but in Europe!

Work to build the reservoirs started in 1853, and was completed by 1904 when the eleventh was finished. The busy Forest Road cuts between them, with three on the north side – Lockwood, High Maynard and Low Maynard – and seven on the south: the East and West Warwick, plus No. 1 through to No. 5.

So, where, I hear you ask, is the eleventh? Well, in 1969 this was remodelled into the Coppermills Water Treatment Works, south of Coppermill Lane. When this reservoir was drained for that work it attracted a flock of Bearded Tits, one of the few records for the site, but with the array of reedbeds now being planted around

Above: Little Egret chicks in the nest at Walthamstow, spied through a telescope.

Opposite: Mute Swans in flight. They have noisy wing beats which you can hear from some distance, unlike the silent wings of Bewick's or Whooper Swans.

the new reserve perhaps they will become frequent visitors. . .

Bearded Tits are just one of a long list of species recorded here at Walthamstow, including an impressive number of rare birds. Over the years I've been coming here I've been fortunate enough to have found Red-footed Falcon, Green-winged Teal and Blue-winged Teal. Hence I have a really soft spot for this old patch of mine.

We'll start with the south section, where you'll find the listed Engine House building accommodating the new visitor centre, including a busy café. In front of you is the No. 1 reservoir, one of many where the Grey Herons have nested: originally, as I understand it, they nested on No.5, before doing the rounds to end up currently on No. 2. They're joined these days by Little Egrets, whose numbers have swelled since they turned up in the early 2000s. No. 2 is the best breeding site for them.

No. 2 and No. 3 are adjacent, and both have islands on them holding breeding wildfowl plus the ubiquitous Common Coot and more hidden Moorhens. Little and Great Crested Grebes can be picked up almost anywhere. The outlet at the southern end of No. 3 is good for Kingfishers, and the bushes are known for migratory birds like Pied Flycatcher.

The two reservoirs east of here, No. 4 and No. 5 are higher up, and have little cover around them: they tend to pull in the odd Common Sandpiper and are favoured by wagtails. No. 5's two islands hold the relocated Cormorant colony, which peaked at over 300 pairs in the early 2000s but has now dropped down to just over 100. Two races of the bird breed here, the *carbo* and *sinensis* (the very white-headed ones in full breeding plumage). Also on the west island gulls breed: in 2016 the Herring and Lesser Black-backed

Above: A Kestrel enjoying a vantage point high up in the old Engine House.

Gulls were joined by a pair of Greater Black-backs.

On the far west side of the Coppermill Stream lie the East and West Warwick reservoirs. The East has an island which was re-landscaped in the late 1990s, and its short vegetation is also ideal for gulls – recently a pair of Black-headed Gulls fledged young on it. A few years ago a Spoonbill lingered here as well. There is an old hide here, which strictly speaking faces the wrong way, but you can still look out across the reservoir and it does provide shelter from the elements.

West of here and the other side of the railway line is the West Warwick reservoir, accessible now only via a tunnel at the north end, which often floods in winter, sometimes to some depth! The long reedbed on its east side gets Reed Warblers and the odd Reed Bunting in summer, and switches them for Water Rails in winter. I did manage to see a Bittern here, but in recent years they have become more regular in the sedge along the Coppermill Stream.

This particular reservoir has a great history of attracting very good birds, from rare grebes, including the last wintering Red-necked Grebe, to a long-staying Common Scoter. It's also a favourite spot for Great Northern Divers. Back in 2009 my father found a Purple Heron here which stayed for nearly a week!

Now we return to the visitor centre, cross Forest Road and enter the north side of the reserve, which is less vegetated and more exposed. But from the highest and deepest reservoir, the Lockwood, you get great views all the way to Alexandra Palace to the west and Docklands to the south. Its grassy banks attract Northern Wheatears, wagtails and pipits during the autumn. This reservoir is good for waders, and perhaps the best for Common Sandpipers. One year a group of Eider duck turned up, and two stayed for most of the winter.

The two Maynard reservoirs both have overflows which hold Moorhens and wagtails when water levels are low enough. The Coppermill Stream starts west of the Low Maynard and runs all the way south through the reserve past the end of the West Warwick. Kingfishers may be seen almost anywhere along it.

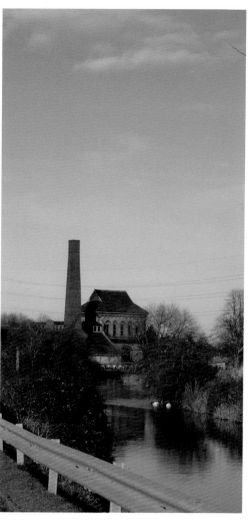

2 Forest Road
London E17 9NH

9.30 a.m. – 5 p.m. daily (Visitor
Centre until 4 p.m)

info@walthamstowwetlands.com
0208 496 2115

Refreshments: café in reserve

Toilets: in reserve

Blackhorse Road (Victoria Line
and Overground); Tottenham Hale
(Victoria Line), 15 minutes

Opposite top right: Greylag Geese are found
not just at Walthamstow but on nearly every
body of water across the capital.

Opposite bottom right: This adult Spoonbill
lingered at Walthamstow for a few days several
years ago, illustrating the atraction this site has
for rare birds.

Right: A sub-adult Gannet. Normally a
sea-dwelling bird, it turned up at Walthamstow
on calm conditions one June, clearly not a well
individual.

As for raptors, Peregrines are frequently seen at Walthamstow,
and on one recent visit in spring I saw no fewer than 11 different
buzzards drifting over! Kestrel can often be spied around the
bottom of No. 3 reservoir, and a number of pairs of Sparrowhawk
breed in the area. Rarer visitors have included Osprey, Red Kite and
Marsh Harrier. House or Sand Martins can occur in large numbers,
which in turn attract Hobbys.

Warbler numbers build up in spring, with Reed Warblers in
almost every patch of waterside vegetation, and Blackcaps and
Whitethroat scattered across the reserve. This is also a great time
to look out for Mediterranean Gulls (March is the peak month), and
April/May is great for Arctic Tern migration.

Walthamstow Wetlands covers a large area, and to cover
it all you'll need to set aside a few hours. These are still working
reservoirs, but as they continue to evolve and be shaped into a
genuine nature reserve, it'll be fascinating to see how its bird
population changes, and hopefully increases.

INDEX OF BIRDS